Wholehearted Me A–Z!

Wholehearted Me A–Z!

Expressions of Wholehearted Living
in Story, Prosetry, and Prayer

Janis Constable
Foreword by Maya Landell

RESOURCE *Publications* · Eugene, Oregon

WHOLEHEARTED ME *A–Z!*
Expressions of Wholehearted Living in Story, Prosetry, and Prayer

Copyright © 2024 Janis Constable. All rights reserved. Except for brief quotations in critical publications or reviews, no part of this book may be reproduced in any manner without prior written permission from the publisher. Write: Permissions, Wipf and Stock Publishers, 199 W. 8th Ave., Suite 3, Eugene, OR 97401.

Resource Publications
An Imprint of Wipf and Stock Publishers
199 W. 8th Ave., Suite 3
Eugene, OR 97401

www.wipfandstock.com

PAPERBACK ISBN: 979-8-3852-1217-0
HARDCOVER ISBN: 979-8-3852-1218-7
EBOOK ISBN: 979-8-3852-1219-4

VERSION NUMBER 030724

Scripture quotations marked NRSV are taken from the New Revised Standard Version Bible, Copyright © 1989 by the National Council of the Churches of Christ in the United States of America. Used by permission. All rights reserved worldwide.

Dedication

In memory of my sister Brenda,
who had an inborn understanding of humanity.
Brenda lived and breathed the Wholehearted Life
with grace, with energy, and with integrity.
Hers was a faith rooted in human kindness and love.

Hers was an enlivened spirit.
Hers was an approach of glass-half-full living.
Thank you, BJ, for leading me, for showing me the way.
I love you Brenda, and I miss you.

Contents

Foreword by Maya Landell | xi
Preface | xiii
Introduction: Understanding Wholeheartedness | xv

Opening Prayer: This | xix

Across the Waters | 1
Attuning | 3
Affirmation | 4

Barnacled Beauty | 5
Becoming | 6
Beloved | 7

Chasing Celtic—The Celtic Consciousness | 8
Color Me—Blessed | 12
Creativity | 16

Dewy-Eyed Dreamer | 17
Deeperlings | 19
Discovery and Discernment | 20

Effervescent Me | 21
Enlivened Soul | 23
Ever-presence | 24

My Faith Identity—Finding Janis | 25
Flâneuse de la Forêt | 28
Freedom | 29

Glass-Half-Full Approach | 31
Generative Spirit | 32
Grace | 34

H-Words and Me | 35
Hearken | 36
Haven | 37

Inherent Integrity—Instilled Integrity | 38
Intrepid Me | 41
Illusion | 42

Journey to Wholeheartedness | 44
Joy | 46
Jabberwocky | 47

Kaleidoscopic Vision | 49
Kindness | 52
Kairos | 53

Liminality—Choosing the Realm of Liminality | 54
Love | 56
Light | 58

Mantle Me, Please | 59
Mystery | 60
Mindful | 60

Nemophilist Noticing | 62
Namaste | 64
Never Alone | 65

Openness | 67
Onward | 68
One | 69

Perseverance | 71
Probably Not Perfect | 72
Prayer Life | 73

Questions | 75
Quiescence | 76
Quaking Quavering Quivering—Not Me | 80

Resourcefulness—Reaching Outward, Inward, Upward | 81
Resilience | 83
Release—Let Go—Let it Go | 84

Sacred Sage of the Soul | 85
Shimmerings | 86
Seeking, Yet Sought | 87

Tough Enough | 89
Truth | 90
Tenacity—This | 91

Uniqueness | 93
Unbridled Mindset—Unbridled Me! | 95
Unconditional Love | 95

Validation through Voices, Vibrance, and Vitreous Lustre | 97
Vocabulary Matters | 100
Vision | 104

Wholehearted Me—Brenda's Light | 105
Wildness | 113
Wisdom | 116

X Marks the Spot | 117
Xyphoid | 119
"Xtraordinary" | 120

Yesterday | 122
YOU-ology | 124
Yearning | 125

Zeal and Zest | 127
Zirconias and Zinnias | 127
Zumba! | 129

Closing Prayer: My Wholehearted Prayer—
My Daily Petition to God of My Heart | 131

Suggested Reading | 133
About the Author | 135
Bibliography | 137

Foreword

When you pick up a book, you are holding a piece of someone's life.

When you pick up this book,
you are holding a piece of someone's heart.

When you pick up a book, you wonder what it might hold for your life.

When you pick up this book,
you are holding an invitation to your own heart.

Wholehearted Me A—Z! is an invitation to witness, explore and learn from Janis Constable's life, her relationship with the Holy, with others, with words, with her past and present, with nature and the world around her. It is an invitation we all need.

As little children we come fresh to the world, trusting, learning, exploring and feeling. We wear our hearts on our sleeves—using our senses to help us know what we really like or do not like. We learn our first letters, which lead to words and then to sentences, which lead to stories that open our hearts to life's possibilities. We come wired for this Wholehearted Living and somehow along the way we get lost. In order to be found, we need to learn our ABC's again. This is an Alphabet to help us remember who we are and whose we are.

Janis' words are an invitation to be found, one letter, one word at a time. Turn to any page and there is something there for rumination, for wonderment, and for each of us to take to heart. Her writing emerges out of the mess of all life—evidence that this wisdom does not come without the human experience of the hard places: loss, grief, despair and wilderness. She writes with an honesty and a hopefulness that summons something out of you. It asks you to awaken to your own life, and to the choices that are right in front of you. She models being all in, taking a path that pays attention, and practices gratitude for what is right in front of her. In this way, she points to life itself.

I come from a tradition that begins a new year with the practice of picking an Epiphany Star Word. You are invited not just to read this book from A—Z but to pick a word—any word—and see how it connects to your life. Whether the words are old friends found in the familiar, or newly written into the world by Janis' creativity, they will find you. May they make a way for freedom, grace and peace to prevail. May they bless you with the courage to live into your worthiness. May they help you to make a path with honesty and openness. Keep coming back to these words and they will help you to write your own story. May they start your Wholehearted chapter.

When you pick up a book, you are holding a story about a part of life.

When you pick up this book,
you are holding a story of Wholehearted Life.

When you pick up a book, you yearn for ancient and new wisdom.

When you pick up this book,
you are holding Wholehearted Wisdom.

May it be So.

Reverend Maya Landell
Islington United Church
Toronto, Ontario, Canada

January 10, 2024

Preface

Greetings fellow journeyers! In *Wholehearted Me A-Z !*, I want to share with you my understanding of Wholehearted Living, not from a social scientist's standpoint, or from a researcher's statistical analysis, but rather, from a wholly different approach—a unique approach—through my own lived experience as expressed in story, prosetry and prayer! You will not be wading through stats and trends and findings and conclusions! Rather, you will find yourself immersed in colorful imagery, contemplative verse and personal prayer.

In the realm of Wholeheartedness, best-selling author Brené Brown admits that she is someone "committed to research that reflects our lived experience"[1], whereas I would assert that I am someone committed to contemplative prose and prayer that reflects our lived experience! And it makes me feel really good to say so—and to share my work with you!

Wholehearted Me A-Z! is written in the first person point of view—I—Me—My. It is my intention to draw you, the reader, in close, closer, *to experience Wholeheartedness* in a most intimate and up-close-and-personal way. It is my intention that you, the reader, will be able to identify easily with me, discovering that we are indeed, on this Journey into Wholeheartedness together!

Uh Oh! Here comes that dreaded double negative sentence structure! Please please please DO NOT choose TO NOT read my work because of its perspective of white female middle-class first-world privilege! Please CHOOSE TO read my work because Wholeheartedness resonates deeply with you! Wholeheartedness has no boundaries or borders—it IS relevant to all people, all cultures, in all places. It IS timeless. And, it most certainly has a place in your life and living.

Along with my desire to be fully open, honest and transparent, I'm hoping that the tone of my written work comes across as friendly,

---

1. Brené Brown, *Atlas of the Heart*, 2021, page 184

Preface

encouraging, and uplifting. The first person point of view does run the risk of seeming self-centeredness and egocentricity. Not intended at all!

Interior Work *is meant to be* proactive, and self-focused self-care! I hope that my own humility and the humbleness of my words—that *both of these* will rise up and shine through. It was most certainly a joy—pure joy—for me to write!

My credentials for writing this book emerge from my very own colorful life experience, out of my desire to share what I've learned along the way, and, out of my firm belief that Wholehearted Living is a most wholesome and centering way of life.

Wholehearted Me A-Z! is approachable prose. It is profoundly experiential, poetic, and relevant. My words are not here *to teach, per se.* Rather they are here for you . . . . *to encounter—to feel and to sense—to experience deeply—to inspire you to embody the Wholehearted Life. Let my words open you fully. May you enter into the oceanic vastness that is the realm of Wholehearted Living! May my words lead you into your own style of contemplative thinking, into curiosity and creative inquiry, and, into many enlightening conversations!*

Janis Constable
February 10, 2023

Introduction

Understanding Wholeheartedness

You might want to ask "Wholeheartedness, the Wholehearted Life, Wholehearted Living all sound so wonderful! But, what are they? What is Wholehearted Living all about?"

Wholehearted Living is an intentional practice which is refined—which comes into fuller clarity—throughout the seasons of life. It is a chosen lifestyle. It is deeply engaged living. It is simply, a way of being.

Wholehearted Living is grounded in many of the tenets of traditional faith practices—Worship of the Divine, love, compassion, respect, peace, harmony, honesty, trust and service—all are key.

Wholehearted Living is mirrored in the sparkling facets of positivity—optimism and glass-half-full-living, self-awareness and affirmation, and a real sense of personal connectedness and belonging.

Poetically speaking, Wholehearted Living is framed in the ultra-fine-grained wood of wholesomeness—in an ornate wooden picture frame carved out by what is good and right, natural, pure and true.

My interpretation of Wholehearted Living differs somewhat from the scholars, the researchers and the best-selling authors, since my own lived experience with Wholeheartedness differs from their studies, data and academic works. The following passages will broaden and deepen your understanding of my personal take!

My Celtic Christian roots are strong, and they certainly influence all of my choices—in my life and in my writing. If I were to name a touchstone, a core truth of Wholehearted Living, I'd weigh in strongly with these centering words—with this teaching from the ancient Celtic Wisdom . . . .

As we are ALL born OF God, we are ALL Sacred. ALL of life is Sacred. And therefore, we intuitively reverence ALL life, ALL form, ALL of Creation, as naturally as we breathe. We are ALL connected—interconnected—through our very Sacredness. We ALL belong, as we are ALL Sacred. We naturally honor the Sacred in one another, simply, by always respecting one another, and by freely showing our love and compassion for one another.

It is my personal belief, that the touchstone of Wholehearted Living, is this genuine Honoring of the Sacred in ALL life and form. When we choose to engage deeply in our own lives, by respecting, loving and showing compassion for one another—all from a stance of true reverence—we are Wholehearted. We are intentionally living the Wholehearted Life.

For me personally, regardless of how my day ends today, tomorrow morning I shall arise knowing I am Sacred, beloved, and called. I will be energized, knowing I am Sacred. I'll move forward, enlivened and full of hope, simply in this knowing. And, I will choose to reverence—I will choose to honor—the Sacred in all life and living, in every moment through all my days. In so doing, I will choose to live out the core truth of Wholehearted Living.

But, this is just the core. There is so much more about Wholeheartedness that I need to share! There's a whole dictionary of vocabulary on the subject. There are colorful definitions. There is perspective and nuance, and of course, there are blurred lines. I have sought out a whole vocabulary—in accessible language—to fully communicate the fire and the finery of Wholehearted Living.

So then you might ask "Is *Wholehearted Me A-Z* really a dictionary?" My short answer—"*Wholehearted Me A-Z* is not a dictionary, so to speak. Rather, metaphorically, it is dictionary for Wholehearted Living! Personified, it lives and breathes Wholeheartedness. In truth, in reality, this book of verse and prayer is the go-to anthology of the Wholehearted Life."

Wholehearted Me A-Z is an alphabetically arranged collection of Story, Prosetry and Prayer—in expressions of my lived experience of Wholehearted Living. It is curated just for you—for you on your chosen journey of Wholehearted Living—for you in your quest of self-understanding and self-affirmation. The Wholehearted Living vocabulary, and the awesome colors and shapes of Wholeheartedness, are illuminated beautifully through the use of allegory, poetic imagery, and petition.

Wholeheartedness appears in contemporary literature through many lenses, contexts, and perspectives. Writers, scholars and poets come to align—*great minds do think alike!* Please read on!

Best-selling Christian author Rachel Held Evans states that "WHOLEHEARTED FAITH lives not in the mental citadel but on the open, windswept plains of the heart" [2] I love the inherent truth of her very real and image-conjuring word choices.

Renowned social scientist Brené Brown concludes in her studies, that "WHOLEHEARTED LIVING is about engaging deeply with our lives from a place of worthiness." [3] I love the juxtaposition—the simplicity and the depth—of her words. I love the relevance of her research findings in my daily living.

And I, contemplative poet Janis Constable, reveal in the vivid colors of my prosetry, that *"WHOLEHEARTED ME is simply a mindset—and a heartset—of the all-in openhearted seeker. Wholehearted Me arises as I reverence the Sacred in others. I am my faith—I am my Wholehearted Living Faith—I am, Wholehearted Me!* I love the reality of these words.

Truth, simplicity, depth, relevance and reality—all to be revealed—all are my intentions in penning this book!

Come! Test the waters and then immerse yourself in Wholehearted Living! Enter into a new and comfortable wordset and wordspace—into a deeper understanding of Wholehearted You! Arise out of the depths of your own nebulous thoughts, owning a new, fresh and clear vision of the Wholehearted Life! Come away from your read, knowing your place in the Wholehearted Life!

I hope you'll be able to say *"I now know what Wholehearted Living looks like, and feels like, and I want this in my life."* May you see, and sense, and feel your way into Wholehearted Living. May the lived experience of Wholeheartedness be yours!

Blessed be your journey into the Wholehearted Life. Amen!

Janis Constable

---

2. Rachel Held Evans, *Wholehearted Faith,* 2022, page 54
3. Brené Brown, *The Gifts of Imperfection,* 2010, page 125

Opening Prayer

This

All life is truly interconnected, and Sacred,
  thanks be to you, God.

With fullness of heart and head
  I walk with you, God,
    through the intricacies of life—
      through the rhythm and rhyme of time—
        through the dark and through the Light.

Wholehearted in approach,
  enlivened in body, mind and spirit,
    I reverence you.
      I reverence all life and all living.
        This is my will.
          This is my joy.
            This be my vision.
              This be my Wholehearted Life.

This be my humble and prayerful offering to you, God,
  now and ever, Amen.

Across the Waters

'Across the Waters' is a dynamic mindset,
    a way of seeing, a way of being.
        It is a true liberation of body mind and spirit.

Fresh new thinking. Revelation.
    No limits, boundaries or restrictions.
        No hoop-jumping or brick walls blocking the way.
            Unbridled consciousness.
                Freedom place and happy place—
                    and happy dance too!

Place yourself in the heights, on the edge, at the precipice,
    looking out into the open—the oceanic wide wide openness.
        Open yourself. Re-invent yourself.
            Re-imagine yourself in Wholehearted Living.

Gazing, dreaming,
    yearning, learning,
        visioning, envisioning.

Longing, belonging,
  connecting, disconnecting,
    part of, more of, reaching out, stepping out.

Emboldening, empowering,
  being, becoming,
    present, graced, One.

Issues, sentiments, questions, conundrums,
  bubble and churn in random-and-nebulous-chaos,
    and emerge with clarity, in Light-bearing truths.

Faith opens. Hope arises.
  Healing begins. Transformation wells and swells.

Light into Light—Across the Waters.

Open the eyes of my soul to see
  within beyond and through—
    the Sacred, the Holy, the real—
      the true.

May I be open and spacious,
  expansive and free.
    With fresh hope arising, the new day is calling ME
      into the truth, into the now,
        into the spaces of life and matter—
          into the vastness across the water.

Across the waters I am. I delight. I shall ever be—
  shimmering, shining. I shall rest—be free.
    Light into Light—so let it be.

Attuning

In the moment, in the present, in the now, simply stop.
   Come into awareness. Notice. Wonder. Appreciate.
     Breathe—breathe deeply.

Explore the details. The process.
   The history. The mystery.
     The truth.

Allow yourself to simply be,
   as you attune to your whereabouts,
     noting your place and your space in the moment.
       Awaken to all life and movement and energy
     beyond your comprehension.

Listen. Listen deeply.
   Attune to vibration.
     Voiceless words.
       Beckonings and callings.
         Feel the palpable rhythms
           and unspoken realms, in your midst.

It is in these intentional moments of attuning,
   of coming to stillness,
     of finding yourself in relation to your surroundings,
       that you open,
         that you grow,
           that you become more than you were.

It is in these moments of attuning,
   in these moments of immersion and complete engagement,
     that you discover and discern, deem and dream,
       that which you need for your understanding.

The practice of attuning is at once ethereal, and real.
   It is time and energy spent on the minutiae of the moment.
     It calls you into mystery, into the Sacred, into Presence.
       It is transcendence for the soul.

Come to the Thin Place.
 Walk on Holy Ground, communing.
  Here, there is no separation or divide
   between the human and the Divine.
    Wholeness. Grace.
     Eternity. One.

Come. Attune. Find your way. See the Light.

Affirmation

Dear God of 'Across the Waters and Beyond', hear my prayer.

I am wide open here, in this place, in this space.
 My mind, my heart, my faith—my whole being—is open.
  With eyes wide open, I survey my surroundings.
   My mindfulness takes me to the cliffs at the shore,
    where the wide open waters ever widen before me,
     where life and dreams and visions alike
      can unfold in the horizons
       way way way out there.

I notice. I attune. I appreciate.
 And I affirm that my wholehearted self
  is here, present, and ready for the journey.
   I affirm that Wholehearted Me is humbled
    by your Presence, by your grace.
     I affirm the wonders of your hand
      in my Wholehearted Living.

God of 'Across the Waters and Beyond',
 I affirm my willing presence here with you. Amen.

Barnacled Beauty

Aging gracefully. Aging graciously.
    Accepting what is, versus, what was.
        No kicking and screaming. No turning back.
            Seeing that wrinkles, roundness, and wisdom
                are trophies won in a race-well-run.

The heavy-boob-stoop, the sparkling white cropped and curly mop,
    the arthritic limp with the compensatory swagger,
        are all prizes earned in the ongoing marathon of life,
            as are the emotional scars, the slowness to trust,
                the excessive baggage of hurt, abandonment,
                    isolation and fear—all of these are mine.
                        I own them all.
                            But, none of them define me.

I wear my barnacles proudly. I do not hide them.
    They are part of me. They are part of my life story.
        They are part of my formation, part of my becoming,
            part of the very essence of my being.

And this barnacled beauty makes no apologies.
   I was born. I have grown and transformed.
      I have been shaped and formed and adorned.
         I have emerged in my wholeness, in my now.
            This is me. Barnacles and all.

Life on the shores, life on the rocks, life with the tides,
   is where my barnacles found me,
      became part of me, became one-with-me.

Barnacled Beauty meets Sailor Bill
   and onward they will
      live happily ever after!
         Age needs no measure
            when barnacles are the treasure, the pleasure, the food.
         Life is good!

Becoming

The dragonfly transforms slowly, from waterborne to airborne.
   The bulb becomes a tiny bud and then a beautiful blossom.
      The cloud of moisture becomes rain
         and it falls to earth to become rivers and lakes and streams.
            They all have their niche. They all have their place.
            They all have their time to shine.

Life begins. Life unfolds.
   Life evolves and morphs and transforms. All life becomes.

I hope that my becoming will be smooth and freeing and meaningful.
   I dare to trust that with my becoming,
      comes a life of purpose and meaning and gift—and service.

I seek to find strength and solace in my being, in my becoming.
    I seek the Sacred in all that I am, in all that I will be.
        I seek that precious perfect peace that comes from God,
            in my knowing, in my growing, in my being with God.

In Popeye-esque affirmative lyrics . . . .
    I'm Janis, the Sacred Child—my spirit is free and wild—
    Wholehearted, becoming, 'cause I am beloved—
    I'm Janis the Sacred Child!

I am becoming the child of God that God calls me to be.
    Thanks be, to God.

Beloved

Dear God, hear my prayer.

On this pathway, on this journey, on this Odyssean passage of mine,
    You are with me, God. You call me beloved, and beloved I am.
        You are the Potter's hand, shaping me and forming me.
            You are shaping me with your love.
                And, I am worthy, barnacles and all. Amen.

Chasing Celtic—The Celtic Consciousness

Following, are just a few tenets of the ancient Celtic Wisdom,
    to set the scene.
        For a more complete understanding and perspective,
            consider reading any of
                author John Philip Newell's books.

They are deep. They are relevant in a seeker's journey.
    As I mentioned already in the Preface,
        I affirm that some of the ancient Celtic Wisdom
            is truly a touchstone—is truly a cornerstone—
                of my own Wholehearted Living.

Connection. Connected. Connectedness. Interconnectedness.
    All from the Latin word, connectere—
        con (together) and nectere (bind)—to be bound together.

    A universal need to be connected, to people, to community, to home.

C

A sense of being drawn to that, which links and joins—
  people, hearts, places, souls, moments, time, eternity, and God.

An ancestral draw—to cherish family roots near and far.

A spiritual quest—calling out to seek the sameness
  in all matter, in all life and living.
    A spiritual quest—seeking to know
      the Sacred in all life, and,
        the Sacred Light within all form and matter.

The Celtic knots and braids were
  intricately interwoven, interlaced, intertwined,
    describing the fluid nature—the flow—
      of connections in their midst.

As highly symbolic handiwork of the harmonies of the seasons,
  of the peace and contentment and love
    flowing within hearts and faith communities,
      these knots were woven, tied, braided—
        defining community and connections of the times.
        These braids wrought strength and hope.

The human race—humans—are not solitary beings.
  They find connection through conversation,
    through working toward workplace common goals,
      through community sports and environmental movements,
        through political advocacy for social justice,
          through worship,
            be it individual or collective practices.

Humans thrive when they choose connection and interconnectedness,
  when they choose compassion and humble service to others in need.

They flourish when they choose connection and interconnectedness,
  when they live in respect with Creation.

All life is not made BY God, rather, all life is OF God.
This simple knowledge intimates—infers—affirms—
the truth of the Sacredness of all life and living.

I am OF God—I am Sacred.
   You are OF God—You are Sacred.
      The trees are Sacred. The waters are Sacred.
         The sun and moon and stars and the wind—all Sacred.
      The Sacred in me honors the Sacred in you.
      Namaste.

In 2019, I traveled to Iona, Scotland, the Holy Isle.
   People say that it is a truly Sacred Place,
      and that you can sense this immediately upon leaving the ferry
      and setting foot on the ancient Hebridean Shores.

In 563 AD, Irish Monk St Columba
   was the first to bring Christianity to Scotland,
      when he landed with his fellow monks
         on Iona's southwestern pebble beach shore.

He found a bleak and barren island. Great fishing.
   Great plains and elevations for sheep and shepherding.
      Iona would soon become a small community of new Christians
         with a passion for wholesome and peaceful living—
      while crofting in a harsh and wilderness land.

I visited the ruins of the nunnery.
   I worshipped communally in the Abbey.
      I spent quiet times by candlelight in solitude and in prayer
         in the ancient St Oran's Chapel.
            It echoed seemingly,
               with the solemn chants of yesteryear.

C

I strolled the white sands on the great northern strands.
   I hiked up the highest hill—Dun I—
      to experience the wonders—
         the mystical wonders of the waters of eternal life
            at the well of St Brigid, in the heights.

I traversed the grassy plains dotted with sheep,
   and I trekked around—circled around—the great soggy bog.
      I ate my boxed lunch on a lofty heather-clad hillock,
         and from there, I could almost see Ireland's shores!

In all of these places, I had the gift of time—the precious gift of time.
   I could immerse myself in the moment—in the Holy Moments.
      I could allow myself to enter deeply into the mystical realm.
         I could allow myself to know
            the Ancient and the Eternal. Selah

Celtic Wisdom scholars often speak of the Thin Places.
   These are not so much physical or geographical locations
      as they are a state of heart or mind
         out in the wilds of Creation,
            in the presence of the Holy,
               the Sacred, the Divine.

With an openness, a readiness and a receptivity of spirit,
   the place—the space—
      the separation between the human and the Divine
         becomes distinctively thin, almost absent.
            The presence of the Divine therein,
               is notable, palpable, and tangible.

It was there on the shores, in the heights, at the well,
   on the hillocks—on the heathered brae—
      that I came to understand
         the true relational essence—
            the Sacred relational essence—
               and the grace of the fair Thin Place.

I came home from my Iona travels as a changed person.
　I've been metaphorically unpacking
　　my transcendence and my own inherent Sacredness,
　　　ever since.

Being able to affirm my identity as a modern Celtic Christian
　is a very large part of my own recent Spiritual Formation Journey.
　　I will continue to study, explore, and experience
　　　the Celtic Wisdom, in my faith journey.

Let's see where this leads me
　in my journey of Wholehearted Me.
　　Let's see where this leads me down the road
　　　as I continue Seeking Sacred and Chasing Celtic,
　　　　as I embrace my emerging Celtic Consciousness. Selah

Color Me—Blessed

Color me 'part of'—
　one-with, integral, connected, interconnected,
　　mosaic, spiral, fractal, order, chaos.
　　　New and fresh. Ancient, yet in season.
　　　Tender, yet tough. Frail and fine.

Isn't it a grand perceptual awakening
　to attune to the interconnectedness of all—
　　from microcosm to macrocosm—
　　　from particulate to cosmic—
　　　　from Human to Divine?!

Isn't it wonderfully freeing, to revel in and to reverence
　the interconnectedness of all?!

C

Isn't it Holy, Divine, Sacred,
   to witness the mystery and the wonder,
      of all parts of the whole—
         of all interconnectedness—
            and to simply let them be—Mystery?!

Might we all open our hearts
   to the wonder and the mystery
      of all that links us together—
         of all that connects us to God—
         of all that connects us in life,
            and in love, and in Light?

Color me driven—
   at work, in the pool, on the field, academically—
      always with a raging hunger and thirst,
         to get things right.

Isn't it just so very energizing to stride out,
   with both eyes—and with heart and mind—
      clearly focused on the target?
         Forward, onward, on point!

Isn't it fulfilling, gratifying, enriching,
   to cross the cherished finish line
      knowing that you had put your whole self out there
         and you went the distance—and the extra mile?

Might we all simply strive, and drive ourselves,
   to work hard, to get it right, to dream big, to soar?

Color me kind—
   compassionate in the ER, and on the street,
      and in the darkened places where very few would even go.

Isn't it just the right thing to do,
  to instinctively reach out, to encourage, to support,
    to be present to, to give, to share—
      with all of those who, in their time of need,
        would never ask for the help
          that they so clearly and desperately need?

Isn't it heartwarming to know in your heart
  that your timely, small act of kindness, generosity or compassion,
    just made a huge world of difference to one darkened soul?

Might we all embody these exquisite words—
  all souls matter?

Color my servant heart—
  in body mind and spirit wholeness,
    as I walk alongside, prayerful and peaceful.

Isn't it a true calling from deep within, to step forward to serve?
  Isn't it the gist of the story—the central appeal—
    in the parable of the Good Samaritan,
      to go out of our way and then some,
        to serve both neighbors and strangers alike
          with a willing servant-heart?

Might we all take up the Scriptures and carry them in our hearts,
  arise and shine—and serve?

Color me deep—
  contemplative, attuned,
    in the moment, here and now, present.

Isn't it an expansive and spacious place to be,
  aware, attending, taking in, sensing, absorbing,
    wondering, questioning, querying—simply being?

C

Isn't it awesome—stirring and moving—
   to take the time to enter into the depths,
      to deep dive into a deeper well of wisdom,
         to dwell there, to be nurtured by appreciative wonder,
            to be momentarily caught up in or even lost in
               the contemplative realm?

Might we all take a moment and enter in,
   and listen for the Light of my words?

Color me whole—
   centered, contented, strong in my faith,
      whole, yet part of something so much bigger than my single self.

Isn't it absolutely completing, knowing that you are ever and always
   befriended and beloved by God?
      In your wholeness, you become one-with-God!

Isn't it simply mysterious, and mystical, in understanding
   that you are OF God,
      that you are Light,
         that you are Sacred?

Might we all take a breath, and take all of these colors into our souls—
   might we all breathe in all of these colors—
      might we all make these colors our very own—
         make them come alive in our colorful wholehearted lives?
            We might then sigh, and speak these words,
               blissed be, blessed be!

Color me blessed—
   color me humble—
      color me grateful—
         thanks be to God! Amen!

Creativity

Creator God, please hear my impassioned and wholehearted prayer.

Cultivate in me—nurture in me—a wild and creative spirit,
   that I may boldly and radically
      use my gifts to reach out, and to show,
         all that I have learned, all that I believe,
            and all that you would have me share.

Please fuel my sharing spirit—my passion to engage my readers—
   in some new and inspiring contemplative works.

Please bless my works—liturgical, musical and poetic—
   that all I create in word and in song
      may pique curiosity, and stir into flame,
         and fire up the joy of creativity in others—
            that my works might then spark
               the wildness of their own creativity
                  freely, broadly, and, joyfully!

Help me to generously shine my creative fire,
   and let me live in its wild and flickering light. Amen.

Dewy-Eyed Dreamer

Allowing waking dreams, visions and out-of-the-box-thinking—
   simply allowing these to percolate, is just the beginning!

Opening self to newness, freshness, uniqueness, originality,
   doesn't come easy for all,
      but it is worth the time and energy,
         the passion and the drive.

Appreciative wonder and listening—deep listening—
   create an openness of mind and a spaciousness of mindset,
      fueling the opportunity to engage most fully in the moment.

When space is created,
   when the limits and pressures of time are removed,
      the creativity flows, the dreaming begins,
         and the ingenuity emerges.
            Transcendence may follow,
               depending on the content of the dream,
                  or vision, or direction of thought.

Wholehearted Me A-Z!

The dewy-eyed dreamer arrives,
  filled with awe, and delight,
    and a certain readiness to follow their own nose.

Wanderlust, reckless abandon,
  random and nebulous thoughts and unbridled thinking
    cascade in the creative space
      in the creative mind
        in the creative time.

Ideas and visions may emerge
  as scattering and bombarding,
    or, as slow and methodical processes.

Give yourself permission to dream.
  Give yourself to dream—to envision.
    Intentionally create space
      for creativity to flow, to flourish,
        to flounce and to flaunt!
          Go with the flow!

Wonder. Delight. Question. Fancy. Dream. All verbs!
  Be the dewy-eyed dreamer who draws outside the lines,
    who delves into, who dances, who dares—
      who opens self to creative self-expression.

Rise up, energized, expressing your innermost self.
  Put yourself out there, in imaginal reverie.
    Showcase the inner you in your visioning.

Make this openness, this broadening, this deepening, this flowing,
  become part of you—become part of your Wholehearted Living.
    You can do this!

Deeperlings

I love to seek out the deeper meanings—deeperlings and Sacred truths.
   I well up with extraordinary delight
      in discovering emerging trends and truths—
         in unearthing and illuminating
            simple buried and overlooked truths.
               I try to simplify, and make sense of it all
                  as I contemplate,
                     poetify and prosify my world.

Deeperlings are little tidbits of truth
   brought forward, outward, and upward into the Light.
      They are profound in their reach,
         and more often than not,
            they are basic truths
               for Wholehearted Living.

Deeperlings arise from within,
   seemingly intuited,
      sometimes surprising,
         most often they are affirming
            the knowledge and wisdom
               carried deep within.

Sacred wisdom—truth—deeperlings—all are carried within us.
   It is our privilege to seek them, find them,
      and unlock their meaning and relevance
         in our own Wholehearted Living.

Listen to Ravenwolf. Seek truth in the brilliance of Brené.
   Identify with Richard and Richard.
      Attend to the teachings of Taylor and Tolle.
         Let Rachel point you toward Wholeheartedness.
            They all know deeperlings, intimately.

Go deep. Make time to go deep and stay there.
 Listen. Attune. Wonder. Let the voiceless voice speak to you.
 Let the Sacred Sage of your Soul call out to you.

Let the wisdom of the ages from deep within you arise,
 and guide your conscious thoughts.
  Let deeperlings nudge you, and nourish you, feeding you
   with the truths you need in your Wholehearted Living.
  Let deeperlings show you more.

Discovery and Discernment

Dear God, hear my prayer.

Oh what a journey! Oh, what a fulfilling journey into Wholehearted Living!
 Help me to discover new and fresh ways and pathways.
  Help me to discern my way forward, in my becoming,
   in my dreaming, in my envisioning, in my listening,
    in my attuning, in my embodying
     of Wholehearted Living. Amen.

Effervescent Me

I met my husband in the 1980's, and we dated for five years.
   It was a lovely journey of getting to know each other,
     in good times and in sad.
        It was a time of being open to each other,
          and learning to trust each other,
            and a time of figuring out
              what made each other tick.

Barry learned early on, that I was one open and friendly soul.
   He frequently commented and marveled at my engaging ways.
     I spoke to anyone and everyone.
       I always felt free to speak to people.
         After all, they were only humans, just like me.

In downtown Toronto, I would talk to store clerks, bank tellers,
   passersby, neighbors, and strangers alike.
     I talked about superficial things and at times,
       I'd enter into random deeper conversations
         of the heart and soul.
           I liked that a lot.

Wholehearted Me A-Z!

My friendliness defined me. My openness revealed me. The real me.
  My trust in humanity gave me permission
    to approach anyone, anytime.
      I was optimistic, joyful, happy, and contented with life.

My spirit was enlivened
  And a certain energy was always bubbling up from within me,
    showcasing my sparkling *joie de vivre*.

Then one day, Barry coined a phrase for my lighthearted way of being.
  He said "You're EFFERVESCENT! You're bubbly!
    You're like a little tablet fizzing away in the tall glass.

You're setting off a continuous stream of bubbles rising!
  You're a cloud of energizing mist arising!
    You are one contagious happy camper!
      Who could help but be energized and enlivened
        and stirred into liveliness when you're around?!"

I laughed it off, humbly deflecting the comment,
  saying that it was just my Maritime roots bubbling forth,
    and that it was just natural for me, to be effervescent!

My way is just the east coast down-home way
  of enjoying people and living with contentment,
    and seeing people just as that—
      friendly, approachable, lighthearted and Wholehearted—
        real down-to-earth people.

They were kind, generous to a fault,
  with a lend-a-helping-hand spirit, always.
    Yup. I was dem and dey were me. Yes, b'ys!

Barry had something inscribed on the inside of my wedding band
  that I didn't get to see until after the marriage ceremony.
    It read 'For my FRVSNT love'.

E

I burst into tears, reading this for the first time.
  Barry knew me—he knew me well—
    and he understood me, and loved me for who I was.
      No need to change me, or improve me,
        or turn me into something I'm not.
          No need to limit my effervescence.

He twinkled and said "Yup. Watch 'er go! Let 'er fizz away!
  Yup, she's mine alright. LOL! That's my EFF-ing wife!"

Enlivened Soul

The dawn breaks and I awake, refreshed, renewed, and ready.
  My soul is enlivened at the thought of a brand new day.

Yesterday is behind me, and today is here.
  Time to stretch myself, physically, emotionally, mentally,
    spiritually—radically and randomly.

Time to awaken all of my senses. Time to grow.
  Time to get my feet on the ground and get this day in motion.
    Time to feed my inquiring spirit.
      Time to center myself, ground myself, and engage myself
        in all that will shape me and form me,
          in body mind and spirit.

Is today a day of quiet contemplation, of silence and soliloquy?
  Is today a brisk walk in the woods
    with an openness to the powers of forest bathing?
      Will I stroll by the stream, noticing, attuning, gazing
        like a comfortable *Flâneuse de la Forêt?*
          Hmmmmm....

Where will this day take my soul?
  Where will my enlivened soul lead me?
    I sigh. I sigh again.
      I breathe deep and release all cares to the world.

Let this day begin.
   Let my Wholehearted Living begin.
      Let my enlivened soul be—simply be.

Ever-presence

Dear God,

You are ever-present to me.
   When I arise, when I lie down, you are with me.[1]
      I know the wonder of your presence.
         I feel the joy of your presence.
            I am heart-warmed at your very presence,
               here with me, always.

I am strengthened. I am encouraged.
   I am lifted up into my day, knowing you are with me.

I am humbled. I am grateful.
   I am honored and privileged in knowing you are with me.

God, my faith is in you, and in you alone.
   My faith leads my every action, and colors my every word.

My servant heart, my compassionate life, my Wholehearted Living—
   all of these come from you, and I humbly say 'thank you'
      as you walk alongside me on my journey,
         as you make your presence known to me,
            day by day, hour by hour,
               moment by moment,
                  in the moment, in the now,
                     in the Light of now. Amen.

---

1. Paraphrase of NRSV Ps 139: 2

My Faith Identity—Finding Janis

I have worshipped in the United Church of Canada all of my life,
   yet, I identify with and I choose to commune with
      the saints and the living saints of Celtic Christianity.

The Celtic 'way of seeing',
   and their 'way of listening and hearing'
      are intrinsically the way of my heart,
         the way of my faith,
            the way of my spiritual life,
               the way of my whole life.

The ancient Celtic expression of unity and oneness with God,
   is my song,
      and I am ever singing,
         ever chanting,
            ever rising up with my song.

My chosen personal journey
   into the music and the poetry of the Holy Lovelight
      has grounded me, has greened me, and, has graced me.

The Holy Lovelight is alive in me
  and it's there for me to share with others—
    to kindle and ignite the Joy of Living Faith
      in all whom I meet.

God is with me.
  I am One-With-God.
    And I am whole,
      and peaceful and contented,
        in this understanding
          and in this truth.

As the River flows,
  and as the Lovelight grows,
    let me always choose God.
      Let my heart always 'see the Sacred in all that lives'.
      Let me sing my song.
        Let me shine my Light—
          the Holy Lovelight of God.

Let all of my good choices
  allow my tender new identity to emerge,
    that I might serve You—
      and serve You well! Amen![1]

In asking the question "Who am I?",
  my brain sets off on so many interesting and intriguing tangents.

Mystically, I would self-define in the extravagant uniqueness of
  Curved Light, *Pavo, et L'Arte*.
    But sadly, only the Physics and Linguistics Scholars,
      and the elite Parfumeurs
        would pay attention
          to my illusive poetic metaphors.

---

1. Janis Constable, *Random and Nebulous—Nuancing the Psalms*, 2021, page 12

F

Sigh. I wish to be so much more inclusive for my audience—
   more-identified-with and more relatable—
     and more human, and accessible.
        Please, please, please, bear with me!!!

From the perspective of the heart,
   I would identify with words
      like compassionate, selfless and loving.

Looking through the nebulous cloud of personhood,
   perhaps the words deep, intense, and focused would float to the top.

In the realm of all things social,
   the words friendly-yet-introverted, and preferring one-on-one, sum me up.

Through the lens of approach,
   open, optimistic, and occasionally opinionated.

In the veil of smoldering darkness, in the well of unspoken depths—
   alone, misunderstood and innately paranoid.

In the light of wholeness, and in the abundance of grace,
   I am blessed, beloved, gifted and graced.

Within the spiritual realm, I am attuned, spacious,
   and seeking the Sacred in all life.
      I am part of something big—something far-far-greater-than myself.

In all things Holy,
   I am born of original blessing,
      born of essential goodness,
         and born of the Holy Lovelight of God.

In all matters, I am whole, centered, content, One.
   And I am full of gratitude
      for being one-with-God,
        for being me,
           for finally at last, finding Janis.
              God knows, I wasn't always 'found'.

Curved Light, *Pavo et L'Arte*
  Poetry, Peacocks and Perfume
    Wisdom, Wonder and Whimsy—
      All are Showings and Sparkles and Shimmers, of me!

Come, spend a moment, and dwell in your own depths,
  and count up all of your colors, and your curves,
    and your complex-qualities-of-you.

Find Wholehearted You! Be playful. Be poignant. Be pithy.
  Seek. Find. And give thanks.

In the fullness of the seasons, in the fullness of time,
  in the fullness of Light, in the fullness of you,
    find yourself,
      name yourself—your Wholehearted Self.
        Come to know and love yourself—
          and give thanks.

Flâneuse de la Forêt

Flâneur—noun.
  A French word describing a gentleman strolling—
    at leisure in the city streets—
      one who, with overt interest and intrigue,
        takes time to notice the minutiae of the moment.

Flâneuse is the *flâneur* re-imagined.
  She is NOT a female version of the *flâneur*,
    rather, she is truly a separate entity altogether.
      Independent. Sure. True to self.

The *flâneuse* affirms that women 'experience and explore'
  in a completely different manner than the *flâneur*—
    in a way that earns her
      her own separate name, flâneuse.

Extrapolating then, a *flâneuse de la forêt*
  is a woman well acquainted with the forests,
    who is comfortable in the realm of forest bathing.
      She wanders, treks, meanders, and all the while is
        noticing, attuning, centering.

Birdsong, babbling brooks and pine needle pathways all consume her.
  Her curiosity is given to sights, sounds,
    and fractalificent surroundings—and whimsy!

I liken myself to a *flâneuse de la forêt*—
  a knowing woman idling in the now. A woman about the woods.
    It is part of my identity, my persona, my self-expression.
      Who I am as a *flâneuse de la forêt*
        is part of who I am as a Wholehearted Person,
          who is leading a Wholehearted Life.
            Enlivened. Engaged. Present. Aware.
              Blessed be the *flâneuse* in me!

Freedom

God of my life and living, hear my prayer.

I live in a first world, full of opportunity,
  full of protected rights and protected freedoms.

I do not take any of this for granted.
  I am humbled to live in such fullness and welcomed security.

I come to you in honesty and humility.
  I do not say 'Please grant me freedom.'

Rather, I say wholeheartedly
  'Thank you for the blessings that freedom has brought
    to my life, to my faith, to my whole personhood.
      I am whole, in body mind and spirit.
        I am whole and free.'

Free to worship. Free to speak.
   Free to be. Free to be me.
      Wholehearted me.

I offer my gratitude—
   I speak my gratitude to you,
      for all of my blessings,
         for all of my freedom. Amen.

Glass-Half-Full Approach

My sister taught me all about glass-half-full living.
    She taught me well. She embodied it.
        She walked through life with a breezy presence.
            She saw the good in people.
                She saw the good in the bad.

Brenda knew instinctively to acknowledge the bad,
    but not to dwell with the bad.
        She always looked for the bright side—
            she chose to look for the bright side.

She worked hard at glass-half-full living.
    She worked hard at living in the Light.
        For her world—her own little world—was dark.

Brenda had limitations and medical conditions
    which would restrict all of her activities of daily living.
        Her life would be cut short by her health issues—
            the doctors predicted that she would not see her
                fortieth birthday, and sad to say,
                    they were right.

At age thirty eight, she passed away peacefully,
  having lived a colorful life, within her limitations.

She didn't grumble or mutter "Why me?"
  or seek attention with "Poor me!"
    Never. Ever.

With grace and integrity,
  Brenda accepted the limitations and restrictions in her life
    and she moved forward, optimistic,
      contented with who she was and where she was in life,
        determined to experience all that life could give her.

Brenda's world was dark, but Brenda herself was Light.
  Her Light shone for all the world to see.
    Her optimism, her gratitude, her *joie de vivre*
      were all shimmering beacons of Light for others.

Brenda knew the powers that glass-half-full living had in her life.
  She was well on her way in a life of Wholehearted Living
    when her time on earth was cut short.

Brenda so wanted to share her positivity with everyone—
  She wanted others to know the joy—the reward—the gift—
    of waking each day and reaching out
      to hold that glass-half-full.
        It was her glass.
          It was hers to behold.
            It was her joy, to own and to share it.

Generative Spirit

In a world where productivity and efficiency are everything—
  in a world where the bottom dollar dictates every outcome—
    in a world that is better at taking than giving—
      these words will be comforting.

G

Generative (adjective)—
  having the power or function
    of generating, originating, producing or reproducing.

Simple. Easy peasy.
  But what does it mean, to have a generative spirit?
    Hmmmmm . . . .

Waxing poetic here.
  As the long cold winter blankets the forest bed,
    forest-life-as-it-once-knew-it stops, and plays dead.
      No green leaves for photosynthesis.
        A summer beehive's seeming antithesis.
          Shorter days and longer nights.
            Darkness lingers longer than night.

And yet . . . .
  Forest life continues
    Winter is a formative time. A generative time.
      It is a time of preparation and readiness.
        It is a time to gather in, to conserve energies.
          It is a time for rest, renewal and re-imagining,
            and hope.

And hope leads us straight to the concept of generative spirit.
  The want, the will, the grace, the readiness,
    to move forward, onward,
      productively, creatively, uniquely—
        this is the work of the generative spirit.

The old adage "Where there's a will, there's a way" comes to mind.

Short and sweet, may we all be like Winter.
  May we move forward in hope and in trust,
    with our generative spirit driving us onward.

May we awaken daily to the wonder—to the rhythm—
  that our generative spirit creates.
    May our Wholehearted Living
      be driven by, be given to,
        our generative spirit!

May our generative spirit stir us daily,
  Winter, Spring, Summer, Fall,
    All.

Grace

Dear God of Grace, hear my prayer.

Grace is a state of heart—a state of being—Grace is a way of life.
  Let me live these words, let me embody them
    in my Wholehearted Living, in my Wholehearted Life. Amen.

H-Words and Me

In the 'heretofore of me'
   I was formed. I was shaped. I was groomed.
      I spent a lot of time in the greening rooms, getting ready.

I was blessed with many
   friends, teachers, mentors and ministers
      who believed in me, who encouraged me,
         who showed me the way to my here and now.

And the 'here and now of me'
   is a really good place.
      I am enlivened by life itself. I am grounded. I am centered.
         I am blessed.
            As I am born OF God, I am Sacred.
           In this moment,
               I am One-with-God.

My Wholehearted Living
   has brought me to this place of contentment.
      I am complete.

In the 'henceforth of me'
   I ask for nothing, but
      God's Presence, God's Grace, and God's Holy Lovelight
         to lead me, on my journey into Wholehearted Living.

Here I am, God.
   Let the 'henceforth of me' unfold before me!

Hearken

Can you hear it?
   Hearken. Listen. Hear the call!

In the silence, in the now,
   in the hallowed curve of here and now,
      just pause, breathe, attend—
         pause, breathe, attend.

Maybe there's a message. Maybe not.

Perhaps a single word will nudge you now,
   and play in your heart and on your heartstrings.
      Perhaps the vibe of the music of the spheres simply sounds.
      Perhaps a voiceless voice speaks or sings out in song.

In this moment, in this space,
   in the warmth of God's grace,
      open yourself to receive.
         Open yourself to believe.

In the darkening times,
   God's Holy Lovelight shines.
      God's still small voice is here for all.
         Hearken. Listen. Hear the call.

Hearken here and now.
   Hearken free. Hearken well.

Haven

God of my heart, hear my prayer.

You are truly my haven, my sanctuary,
   my shelter in the storm.

In the chaos, in the dark, in the unknown,
   you are my solace, my comfort, my calm.

In the moment of my living,
   you are my very breath.

I come to you seeking.
   I come to you knowing.
     I come to you humbly.
       Hear my prayer.
         Know my heart.
           Haven my soul. Amen.

Inherent Integrity—Instilled Integrity

Ancient Celtic Wisdom differs from Christianity,
   on a few key teachings.
      Whereas Christians are taught that we are born of Original Sin,
         Celtic Wisdom teaches the very opposite.

Since we are all born OF God—not made BY God—
   then, as God is good, so too we are good.
      As God is Light, so too we are Light.
         As God is Sacred, so too we are Sacred.
            All life and living is therefore, Sacred.

Notably, the Celtic tradition upholds
   that we are born of Essential Goodness, of Original Blessing.

This teaching alone, is so very freeing.
   To know that we are OF God,
      that we are Light,
         that we are Sacred,
            puts a whole new perspective
               on who we are in the universe.

I

It sheds a positive Light on our very being.
  It tells us, that we have an inherent integrity,
    an innate worthiness (some will dislike my choice of word here!),
    an inborn intuition with our God.

I personally believe that integrity is a cornerstone
  in life, in faith, in love.
    Without integrity, the core, the matrix of self
      is shaky, seems vulnerable and inconsistent.
        We lose our value—we are perceived as weak—
          and confidence is lost in its absence.

And I believe firmly,
  that integrity is one of the largest building blocks
    of Wholehearted Living.

We can't be grounded without integrity.
  We can't be centered without integrity.
    We cannot feel connected
      when our integrity falters, or falls down.
        We feel disconnected and insecure
          in our un-integral ways.

Look inward.
  Ask yourself some key questions about your integrity.
    Am I feeling insecure? Why? What about me needs to change?

Am I confident? What is getting in the way of my confidence?
  What do I need to change about me
    to bring me back to strength and confidence?

Am I on the right path, with the right people,
  advocating for the right, the good, the truth?
    What path is the right path? Who are my better supports?
      Do I uphold what is right and good and true?

Am I perpetually finding my own way, stumbling along,
  or am I listening for guidance,
    from God, from intuited wisdom deep within,
      from the wisdom of the earth,
        and walking solidly forward with integrity?
          How do I listen better for guidance?
            How do I re-imagine me?

Take time to reflect deeply on this.
  Let your reflections bring you new insights. New truths.
  Let them lead you to a new and vibrant you!

In my personal world of Wholehearted Living,
  I name *Honoring the Sacred in all life,*
    as the first cornerstone, the first touchstone,
      the first core truth of Wholehearted Living.
        Love follows as a close second (look ahead under L!)
        And *Integrity* is third.
          These three are key. These three are a must.
            These three will keep me strong,
              sturdy and steadfast in my journey.

P.S.,
Trust would be fourth,
  if I were to continue on this numbering train of thought!

P.P.S.,
  My father, Buddy, was a man of integrity.
    He was a great dad and he dearly loved his family.
      His faith was strong and he loved God.

He was ambitious only in that he would do anything
  to provide for his wee family—his wife and two daughters.

He always kept his eyes on the future.
  He had visions, and big bold dreams
    for the family life that we would build together.

I

My dad taught me so much,
    both in his intentional lessons for me throughout my life,
        and incidentally, by his lived example.

I looked up to him as a strong and well-rounded man.
    I turned to him for insight, wisdom, and direction—
        for comfort and encouragement, and for love—
            for his unconditional love.

My as yet unpublished manuscript, titled
    Buddy's Daughter in Soulscape—
        Story Commentary and Affirmations of a Life Well-Lived,
            is a collection of contemplative prose,
                each ending with Amen.

It is a tribute to my amazing dad, and all of his influences on me—
    in my personhood, my attitudes, in my faith,
        in my life, and in all of my life choices.

I wish that all daughters—all sons and daughters—
    could have a close relationship with their father, like I did.

I'm grateful that my dad understood deep down in his heart,
    all the colors and curves and corners of Wholeheartedness.

I am grateful to have been shaped, molded, formed,
    guided, led and loved, by a father whose middle initial
        should be "I"—a capital I for Integrity!

Intrepid Me

Arising in me daily is a strength, a conviction, a power,
    an energy to keep moving forward, to face what lies ahead,
        to motor through,
             to rise up and meet the challenges of the day, of life.

And I ask, where does this come from?
 Was I born with an intrepid spirit?
  Was I always this intentional and forward about conquering,
   or, did something in me evolve, morph, become,
    that I can be this tower of fearless,
     confident, progressive power?

Did all of this come from my glass-half-full approach?
 Did I learn it through my academic world?

Did I emulate these qualities,
 having seen them in other Wholehearted persons?

When I spend time in this question, in a deeply contemplative sit,
 I realize that my intrepidness—my intrepidity—
  arises out of my faith—my faith in God.

For all that my faith has taught me,
 for all that I have embodied through my Celtic Christian faith,
  I stand tall and strong, and arising in me is my intrepid spirit,
   every day, every moment, every here and now.
    Such a blessing. Such a gift. Such gratitude.

Illusion

Dear God of Wisdom of the Ages, speak to me, I pray.

I am learning. I am growing. I am becoming.
 I am reaching out to the scholars of ancient Celtic Wisdom,
  to scientists in Social Humanities Research,
   to authors of Christian-based best-selling books
    on Wholehearted Living.

I approach my quest with optimism, with eyes wide open,
 with heart and faith wide open.

I

I read. I study.
   I listen. I take to heart.
      I embody.

Please assure me—please reassure me—
   that I am on a right path, a good path, a worthy path,
      which will lead me to be
         the Wholehearted child of God
            that you have called me to be.

Please tell me that this is all good.
   Please let me know
      that the promise, the concept and the reality
         of Wholehearted Living is not an illusion,
            that it is truly your works
               through the hands of the scholars,
                  the scientists and the authors.
                     I am listening. Amen.

Journey to Wholeheartedness

The road is long, twisted,
   sometimes easy traveling,
      sometimes arduous and just damn hard work.

The journey can be planned or random,
   straightforward or confusing.
      It can be the long way around
         with plenty of sightseeing and beautiful vistas,
            or it can be a true shortcut—direct and timely.

Whatever be your path—chosen, given or happenstance—
   it becomes a journey
      when there is learning
         when there is growth
            when there are obstacles conquered
               and timelines and deadlines are met.

Whether you travel alone, or in company of friends or strangers,
   you simply move forward, onward, toward your destination.
      Movement, motion, inertia, energy, are all involved.

J

A journey into Wholeheartedness is no different than other travels.
   There is a destination in mind—Wholehearted Living.
      There are markers and measures along the way.
         There are glorious places and amazing people and fun times.
            There are struggles, and misgivings, and doubts.
         There are friends on the journey.

And God is there as your friend, your Sherpa guide, your encourager,
   your teacher, your guru, your Light, your go-to,
      your shoulder, your reason for being, your everything.

The journey into Wholeheartedness is enlivening.
   It is a quest. An Odyssey. A road to becoming.
      A path of emergence. A highway to Wholehearted Living.

How to begin? Begin by soul-searching! By doing a deep dive into you!
   And by reflecting, discovering who you really are.

Assess. Who do you want to be?
   Look at others whom you respect
      and see how you might emulate their ways,
         or learn from their experiences.

Plan. Then set some goals
   Some measureable goals. Some learning goals. Some action goals.

Implement. Do some reading, some studying, some praying.
   Give yourself time to put all of your studies in perspective.
      And then, put you new knowledge into action!

Evaluate. On reflecting over your efforts on your journey,
   you can readjust yourself or readjust your goals.
      Soon you'll have a clear picture of Wholeheartedness,
         of Wholehearted Living,
            of Wholehearted Faith.

This passage was not intended
   to sound preachy, mechanical, or technical.
      But it became just that!

So, now I turn to my world of imagery, and poetic metaphor.
  The journey into Wholeheartedness
    is a gift, a blessing, an honor
      for those who travel the distance,
        for those who are open to learn and to grow,
          for those who wish to draw closer to God,
            and feel more connected
              in their wonderful world.

Journey on, journey strong, journey away, away, and beyond.
  Let the journey form you, reform you, inform you.
    Blessed be your journey. Blessed be you. Blessed be.

Joy

Joy—eternal, ever-present,
  all-perfusing and totally immersive for the ready in spirit.

An internal state, a state of being, a state of heart.
  An elevated and arising state of being, of consciousness, of self.
    An effervescence of innermost emotion.
      A cresting salty tidal swell arising from oceanic depths.
        A volcanic fiery passion—energized and enlivened.
          A mountaintop moment—an epiphanic moment,
            which carries, holds,
              and buoys up continually.
            A freeing sense,
              a liberating breath,
                a presence.
                  God.

Can be shared with receptive hearts.
  Can be lost, can be found, by seeking souls.
    Can be cherished. Can be claimed.

It is warm. It is welcomed. It is invitational. It is contagious.
  It can be overwhelming in a really good way!

J

Know the joy. Feel the joy. Embody the joy. Live the joy. Be the joy.
   Have fun with this one—with this fun-filled musical lexical newbie . . . .
      with a twinkle and a nod, to Mary Poppins and to God!!!
         Joy = Omni-mundi-effervescent-sparklescent-fervor!!!

Jabberwocky

Dear God, hear my playful prayer!

Let the words I speak, and the words I write,
   be meaningful, carry weight, and cause folks to think, to ponder,
      to reflect on their relevance in their own lives.

My fervent prayer is that the intensity of my word
   is heard, is felt, is understood.
      My fervent prayer is that folks take the time
         to dwell in my words, to sit with them,
            to engage deeply in them.

If the readers are in a hurry, or they are a little bit skeptical,
   or judgmental or reticent,
      they will scoff and label my work and call it names.
         Here are just a few of note . . . .

Dogmatic flapjack, self-indulgent twaddle, tommyrot,
   bunk, blather, baloney, balderdash, bellywash, hogwash, gibberish,
      gobbledygook, jabberwocky, mumbo jumbo, word salad,
         And I'm sure there's more—a lot more!

Dear God,

Allow my words—even my exquisite portmanteaus—
   to be heard, to be welcomed, to be understood, to be cherished.
      I love my work. I love my writing. I love to share my writing.
         I pray that readers take heart, take heed, take note.

I pray they find the deeperlings.
   I want them to experience fractalificence,
      and see and feel the kaleidurreal moments.
         I hope that their Metaform meets Metamystique,
            that their Metapresence meets Metanow.

(N.B., Spellcheck is "red-underlining" ALL of these words right now.
   Of course these words won't be found in any dictionary,
      only in my creative wordspace—in my creative realm!)

I pray they understand, that they will grow in understanding.
   I pray that they can lose their judgment of my work as jabberwocky,
      that they can truly see the Light of my words. Amen.

Kaleidoscopic Vision

I'm having an idle moment. Right here. Right now.
   I'm between things on my to-do list.
      I just want to stop and be.
         I sit down in my La-Z-Boy rocker
            and I gaze out the floor-to-ceiling window,
               into the evening.

The woods are dark. Nothing to see out there. Sigh.
   I look over toward the piano and recall
      the spirited medleys and folk tunes and hymns
         played there, over the years.
            This broadens my smile. And I pause.

I look at the bookcase and notice all the new books
   stacked up on the left hand side of the top shelf,
      each of them waiting with baited breath,
         hoping that they particularly will be my next pick,
            my next choice, my next full immersion study.
               I sigh again, quite audibly.
                  I just want to be still.

Wholehearted Me A-Z!

I turn and look at my playlist.
  Sheep May Safely Graze by J S Bach is up next, and I let it play,
    with its peaceful, pastoral melody lifting up up and away
      in my cozy family room—in my wintertime comfort-place.

Maybe I should light a fire in the fireplace.
  No. I'll light a candle instead.
    The Patchouli candle fragrance has a way
      of gathering me in, of collecting me, of centering my soul—
      of filling up my senses and bringing me into stillness.

Done! I can sit back and just chill here, in the moment, calm serene,
  but still very aware and very present.

I look over to the shelf to my right. Lots of 'things' are there.
  The kaleidoscope catches my eye and I immediately reach for it.
    It's old. It squeaks a little in its turning. And of course, it rattles!
      I feel the weight of it in my hand
        and I wonder just how many times
          it has turned around inside over and over and over.

I wonder how many folks have found pleasure in this artful wonder.
  I wonder how many smiles grew and beamed
    just in the thought of its inner workings.

And then, my mind goes deeper. Way way deeper.
  Contemplative mode . . . .
    I begin to draw some parallels of the kaleidoscope,
      and the folks who appreciate its art-form.
        My analysis begins.

Kaleidoscopers are willing to watch
  for trends and patterns, and beauty.
    They are willing to witness change, right before their eyes.
      Perhaps even, by just turning the scope, they are willing
        to initiate change, and to see where things go,
          beyond their control.

K

They are willing to take time to savor beauty,
    and to spend idle time in wonder and awe and anticipation.
        And, as they witness the evolving patterns,
            they are not shouting . . . .

"Slow down! Stop the kaleidoscope! I'll never see THAT pattern again!
    I want to keep THAT one. I want to own THAT one.
        I have to have THAT one! Stop I say!"

Sounds a little silly, a little trite, a little oversimplified,
    until we look at our own lives—
        our own wants and desires—
            and our own needs to have THAT one.

Really good kaleidoscopers
    witness, appreciate, value and 'let go'
        all in the nanoseconds of each kaleidoscopic turn.

Champion or seasoned kaleidoscopers
    are willing to be carried into the moment—
        and they let the colors and patterns speak to their heart, to their soul,
            to their creative spirit.
            They let the colors and patterns
                sneak into their awe and wonderment.
                    They let the colors and patterns pique their curiosity.
                        They understand the domain of Kaleidurreal.

They in turn feel. They engage. They become.
    They gain fresh new perspective on whatever comes to mind,
        all because the kaleidoscope brought them into spaciousness,
            into a certain expansiveness of their whole being.

And then, the kaleidoscoper sets the scope down in their lap,
    and they continue to drift in their spaciousness.
        They see differently, in the moment.

Perhaps they are ready to create something.
　Perhaps they have a new perspective and at long last,
　　they can put two and two together in a whole new way.
　　　Perhaps in their softened state,
　　　　they are ready to forgive,
　　　　　ready to receive,
　　　　　　ready for whatever life brings their way.

Take time. Find your old kaleidoscope.
　In your new kaleidoscopic vision,
　　watch, witness, behold, be free, let go, evolve, create, renew,
　　　become, transcend, be.

Kindness

Kindness is, as a gentle brush of a silken scarf across the arm.
　Soft. Unexpected. Brief but lasting. And memorable. So memorable.
　　The receiver's tactile response continues,
　　　like ripples on a still pond.
　　　　Welcomed. Warming. Needed.
　　　　　The external brush creates an internal rush—
　　　　　　enlivened and heightened awareness—
　　　　　　　as with being lit up and luminescent.

May our own kind words, our actions, and our prayers,
　be as that unexpected silken brush, that moment of softness,
　　that brief attuning, that momentary internal rush of delight,
　　　for the receiver, for the someone in need.

May kindness guide us. May kindness teach us.
　May our kindness rise up naturally, freely, tenderly,
　　through all our days, in all our ways.
　　　In our giving, we receive.
　　　　May our kindness ever reach out as such.
　　　　　Might we, may we always and ever be—
　　　　　　the kindness touch—that silken touch.

K

Kairos

Dear God,

The time is now. Kairos. It is the right time. The opportune time.
   My God-given time for Wholehearted Living.
      May I own this imperative.
         May I make it come into being,
            and into my truth. Amen.

Liminality—Choosing the Realm of Liminality

Realm of Liminality
 is simply a transitional time
  between the old and the new,
   where the old order is lost
    and the new transformation has not yet begun.
     It is found, balanced, on the threshold of change.

Liminality is a time of fresh malleability, and readiness.

In my emergence as a Celtic Christian,
 I have chosen to enter the Realm of Liminality,
  as I re-open my eyes, my ears, and my heart,
   to 'the way of seeing'—
    to that with which I was born.

My eager and ready and optimistic transformation
 is energized from a deep yearning
  to acknowledge the true soul that I am.
   And that indeed is a beloved child of God,
    called to serve in Christ-like living.

L

On my quiet quest into Holiness-and-Christ-like-living,
   I have entered into the Liminal Realm of Transformation,
     and into the Realm of Liminal Thinking.

And I choose to look deep within me,
   to the very center of my being,
     for inner wisdom, insight and guidance,
        in the re-shaping and the re-turning of my faith,
          my heart, and my all.

I choose to listen to, and attune to
   the Voices of the ancient Celtic Wisdom
     that bring me to new doorways and to new thresholds
       of my tender Living Faith.

I also choose to turn to the writings of the Spiritual Masters,
   whose deep faith and critical thinking and contemplative journeys
     guide me in my ongoing Spiritual Formation and transformation.

My life is a string of lovely lustrous Liminal Pearls which 'grace me'.
   As a pearl necklace would grace the neck and visage of a woman
     so too, do my Liminal Moments
       'grace me' with their special place in my soul.
         Liminal Places and Spaces—
           are fresh, new, boundless—and real.

My time in the Realm of Liminality
   is my own personal greening time,
     and my own personal greening space—
       a choice made for me, by me.

To be free to make such life-changing choices
   is both an honor and a privilege.

May I ever and always, choose so well.
   May I emerge, in Liminal Grace. Selah[1]

---

1. Janis Constable, *Random and Nebulous—Nuancing the Psalms*, 2021, page 10

Love

Love—the unfinished masterpiece of the heart—
   the poetry, art, and song of its depths—
      whose canvas is luminous
         whose form can be lustfully lyrical,
            whose harmonies lull, lift, and linger.
               Exquisite and bespoke,
                  yet, universal and common.

Love—in its simplicity—
   is the quintessential glue of life—
      the de facto gel of relational passion—
         the *'je ne sais quoi bond'* of heart-borne bliss.

Love—in its complexity—
   has many vibrant and distinctive faces—
      Philia, Pragma, Storge, Eros, Ludus, Mania, Philautia, and Agape!

Wholesome, welcomed and warm.
   Cherished, coveted, craved.
      Dreamt of, driven by, and dear.

Quivering, shivering, fervent and free.
   Arising from within—
      deep deep deep within,
         yet seemingly and somehow
            external, enveloping, embracing—
               and all-consuming.

Rightfully rash or brash.
   Rarely random—normally nebulous in the now.

Holding—securely, yet gently.
   Holding—yet freeing.

Swept-off-your-feet, yet, totally grounded and sure.
   Fluid—dynamic, evolving and becoming,
      yet solid and constant—steady and true.

L

Sweetly sensorial, like the intimacy of full immersion.
   Palpable, like the chest-pounding thrill of decibelic surround sound.
      Enlivened in every breath.

Rendering moments of tenderness, breathlessness,
   completeness and oneness. Selah

Predictably impetuous in the youth.
   Exhilarating, like the rush and the blush of victory.
      Strong, like sunshine—solar rays at noon in June.
         Feisty-and-protective like a mom for her very young.

Romanced by the sound of the Eternal,
   and the music of the spheres,
      in the river of life,
         in Grand-Canyon-moments,
            in moonlight over waters,
               and in the Northern celestial twilight dance
                  of the Aurora Borealis.

Mystical and surreal,
   yet tangible and real.

Presents itself as *Wordless Knowing Presence*
   emerging in a heartwarming Showing—
      a Shimmering, a Glimmering, a Glowing. Selah

Most Integral Fractal of Holy Lovelight—
given and graced by God.

Always there, for the ready.
   Always there, for the open and receptive.
      Always and ever, love is.
         Always and ever, God is.
            Always and ever, God is love.

Like a canyon, like a crater, like an ocean, like a well—love is.[2]

---

2. Janis Constable "Random and Nebulous—Nuancing the Psalms", 2021, page 177

Light

Dear God of Holy Lovelight, hear my affirmations in prayer.

You come to me God, as Light,
  as a showing of Light,
    in your glowing Holy Lovelight.

I see it. I feel it. I know it. I am it.
  For I too, am Light.

Your Holy Lovelight shines upon me
  and shines within me, in
    iridescence,
      sparklescence,
        adularescence,
          and, in luminescence.

Light arises—it glimmers and shimmers—and graces my very being.

I live in the Light.
  I shine my Light.
    I am Light.
      So be it. So let it be. Amen.

Mantle Me, Please

In the dark, in the drought, I face my fears and my doubts.
   I wrestle. I wait. I wonder.
      Mantle me with hope.

In the strange, the unknown, I wander alone.
   Keep me strong. Keep me safe. Keep me shining.
      Mantle me with Light.

In the day, in my plans, in the challenges at hand,
   I seek purpose, and affirmation.
      Mantle me with meaning.

In the chaos and the noise, in the swell, in the dell, I cringe.
   Mantle me with peace—
      deep deep peace of the running wave.[1]

In the hush, in the rush, my heart is chilling, I need filling.
   Mantle me with love.

I am safe, I am strong, I am free—free to be Wholehearted me,
   with you, God, as my mantle.

    1. Author Unknown, Ancient Celtic Blessing "Deep Peace of the Running Wave to You"

Mystery

Mystery calls.
  Questions with no answers.
    Truth with no proof.
      History versus story.
        Misconception and perceptions.

Like a nebulous cloud of smoldering smoke
  shape-shifting over the embers of the campfire at nightfall.

Like the tide rolling in, brimming, roiling, cresting, questing,
  only to recede into oblivion.

Like a twinkling star in the moonless night
  which suddenly fades to dark, with nary a cloud visible in the sky.

Like the wolf-pack howling at the harvest moon.

Like the dance of the great Northern Lights—
  the Aurora Borealis' wintertime celestial Lightshow.

Mystery. See it. Sense it. Celebrate it.
  Let it be. Just let it be, mystery.

Mindful

Dear God, hear my prayer.

No egocentricity here. Nope. Not here. Not me.
  Simply inward and prayerful reflections.
    Simply mindful interior work.
      Simply focused inquiry in humble mindfulness.

I am mindful of my place—
  in my family, in my community, and in my church family.
    I am mindful of the wonders of my wholehearted approach,
      in all of my relationships.

I take care to nurture these important relationships,
  And I hold all of them in my prayers.

I am mindful of those without a voice,
  of those without the bare necessities,
    of those in dangerous times and places.

My mindfulness leads me into prayer—
  prayers of care and concern, prayers of petition,
    prayers of hope.

I am mindful of the whole of humanity, and its changing emphases.
  There is much indifference, contempt, entitlement and greed
    obscuring the love, the compassion, the respect, and the needs.
      I pray for the renewal and the healing of humanity.

I am mindful of our precious earth.
  She is suffering in our careless hands.
    I pray for better stewardship and better awareness,
      and better political motivations and actions.

I am mindful of you, God,
  and I am so very aware of your ever-presence in my life.
    You are with me. You are the Light within me.
      We are One.

I offer my thoughts—my mindful prayers.
  I speak with humility, with gratitude, with love. Amen.

Nemophilist Noticing

A person who enjoys—and who holds affections for—the forest,
  is a nemophilist.
    It's a Greek word that has been around for a really long time,
      but has only recently come back
        into our contemporary vocabulary.
          Nemos (grove) and philos (affection)
            are the root words.

Forest bathing is a concept originating from Japan, in the 1980's.
  It is known as *Shinrin Yoku* (taking in the forest atmosphere).
    One experiences calm and quiet while being amongst the trees.
    One observes nature and breathes more deeply,
      de-stressing the body mind and spirit,
        and boosting health and well-being.
          A most natural way
            to return to a healthy being—
              to cultivate or restore balance in daily living.

The term appreciative wonder probably best sums up
  both Nemophilist and Forest Bathing
    when specifically referring to a forest setting.

Have you ever intentionally headed for the forest—
   intentionally taken a path through the woods
      with the sole purpose of slowing down and noticing—
         with the desire to simply slow down
            and be in a lush and green and natural space—
               with the intent of communing and being,
                  in nature?

Did you enjoy this? Did you do it again and again?
   Did you feel renewed, refreshed, revitalized, healed?
      Did you sleep better that night?

Then, you already know firsthand the wonders of forest bathing,
   of being a nemophilist,
      of engaging deeply in appreciative wonder in the forest.

I wrote a book, a contemplative novel in 2022, *Light Beyond the River*,
   where the protagonist, Lyra,
      went for a day-long hike in the woods near her home,
         with the sole purpose of clearing her mind,
            of putting out the fire in her head.

She learned some profound life lessons
   from a motley crew of Celtic animals and birds—and a fish!
      She returned home, forever changed.

Her forest bathing, her time as a nemophilist and a *flâneuse de la forêt*
   brought her into the depths of appreciative wonder,
      and she transcended body mind and spirit
         in some most wholesome ways.

In Wholehearted Living—in living the Wholehearted Life—
   attuning and awareness and observation in everyday living,
      are all parts of the whole.

Knowing your place and your space,
   and having your finger on the pulse of your surroundings—
      appreciating the life-giving heartbeat of the moment—
         intuiting the soul of the scene—
            all of these are desired practices,
               dare I say best practices,
                  in Wholehearted Living.

Take note. Notice—notice in the now!

Namaste

Namaste—The Sacred in me honors the Sacred in you.

Such a wholesome approach.
   Such an open and honest greeting.
      Such a positive place to begin time together,
         when the tone—the scene—
            is set with these heartfelt words.

The Namaste gesture is a sign of respect, deep respect,
   a symbol of peace,
      an offering of openness and surrender to the other.

Hands placed prayerfully in front of the chest,
   while bending or bowing slightly forward with eyes closed,
      while offering the word Namaste,
         are common practices in the Namaste greeting.

Oh, that every connection we make, verbal or non-verbal,
   could reach out—reach in—reach toward—
      the shared Sacredness in our midst.

We might breathe easier, feel safer, feel more valued,
   if we all knew that every connection that we made
     in our everyday living—verbal or non-verbal—
       was born of reverence,
         arose out of respect,
           and was guided gently
              on the wings of love and compassion—
                 on the wings of a Servant Heart.

We might all come to know
   what living in harmony, in unity, in peace, really looks like,
     if we are always always always
       seeking the Sacred in 'the other'
         with respect, compassion and love.

May the world reclothe itself in reverence,
   one Namaste at a time.

Never Alone

Dear God of Ever-presence, hear my prayer.

"We are not alone. We live in God's world."[1]
   are the opening words of the United Church of Canada Creed.

They are stirring words. They are comforting words.
   They are words of conviction,
     affirming the truth and the reality
       that God's presence, with us, among us, in us,
         is eternal.
           The ancient word omnipresent
             works well here.
               So does ubiquitous.

---

1. United Church of Canada, *A New Creed*, 1994, page 25

And I embody these words, Wholeheartedly, as if I wrote them myself.
I intuit these words, as if they are arising from the depths within,
arising in the ancient wisdom of the ages
that flows in the eternal river, deep within me.

Dear God-with-me,
I am not alone. I am never alone. I will never be alone.
This is your grace. This is your way. This is your will.
And I am ever grateful. Amen.

Openness

At risk of sounding repetitive, I wrote a book in 2022, a novel,
   Light Beyond the River,
      which showcases the concept of openness, perfectly.

The protagonist Lyra, meets seven Celtic symbolic creatures,
   all of whom have a special life lesson for her.
      But first, for each creature, she must open something.
         Lyra learns the power of being open—
            open eyes, open mind, open heart, open faith,
               open to trust, open to creativity, open to God.

Being open is an intentional practice.
   It is a chosen lifestyle.
      It is engaged living.
         It is simply, a way of being.

Sound familiar?!
   These are the exact words written in the Preface of this book,
      detailing the concept of Wholehearted Living!
         Of course, openness and being open,
            are a very big part of Wholehearted Living!

Being intentionally open,
  having a spaciousness of presence, an expansiveness of mindset,
    and a wholesome readiness—
      to approach, to ask, to receive, to wonder, to contemplate,
        to learn, to experience, to embody, to believe, to grow,
          to risk, to change, to transform, to transcend—
            all of this is part of Wholehearted Living.

The open self becomes a sponge, becomes a magnet,
  becomes a source of newness, freshness, energy and will.
    The open self has conviction and can affirm
      their person, their place and space, in time.

The open self feels connected, interconnected, part of,
  and chooses to stand tall, stand strong, stand true to self.
    This is all feel-good prose. And it's real. It is truth.

If "a Life of Faith can be likened to a life of holy curiosity"[1]
  then by extrapolation, perhaps equally
    'a Wholehearted Life can be likened to
      a life of openhearted and exquisite curiosity!' Selah

Go ahead!
  Open yourself and see what this brings you
    on your journey into Wholehearted Living!
      Seek to discern the place of openheartedness
        in a Wholehearted Life!

Onward

The earth keeps turning, and the days keep dawning.
  The tides rise and fall and the winds blow across the lands.
    There is inertia, motion, energy.

---

[1]. Rachel Held Evans, *Wholehearted Faith*, 2022, page 53

O

It is all around us,
   would we attune to its presence,
      would we even notice its interplay in our lives.

Life is ever moving forward, onward.
   Time on the clock, the tick and the tock, rock on.

And we are all part of this motion, this energy, this earthy inertia.
   We are all acquainted with 'onward'.
      We are all part of 'onward'.
         We can choose to embody 'onward' in our daily approach.

We can even spin 'onward' into positivity,
   just by the energy of our voice,
      the tone of our voice,
         and the urgency of our voice!
            ONWARD!!!

'Non-onward talk' sounds like
   procrastination, resistance to what is,
      negativity, fear, fear of the unknown,
         lashing out and going our own way
            and finding our own way, alone.

Let 'onward' be part of your mantra.
   Let 'onward' start your day.
      Let 'onward' keep moving you forward
         toward Wholehearted Living.

One

Dear God,

I'll sing to you God, a prayerful song.
   The melody may be old and familiar
      but these new lyrics are truly affirming
         for my life, for my faith, for my whole being.
            They affirm my awesome relationship with you, my God.

I am One in the Spirit, I am One with my God,
  And I pray that Wholeheartedness will ground my soul, my all.

And they'll know I'm Wholehearted—that I'm One, that I'm One,
  Yes they'll know I'm Wholehearted—I am One! Amen.

Perseverance

1 Another brick wall? *Yikes!*
  2 Another steep hill? *OMG!*
    3 Delayed? Again? *Whaaaaat?!*
      4 It broke? *Now what?!*

VERSUS,

1 A brick wall?
  I can climb this wall too—*the last one was tough but I managed!*

2 A steep hill?
  The road is definitely going up—
    that means we are getting closer and closer to the top!

3 A delay is okay—*really, it is fine.*
  I can use the extra time to my advantage. No problem. I can do this!

4 Broken schmoken! *I can fix this! I will fix this!*
  I'll find a way to MacGyver it back into top working form!
    And I can just keep on keepin' on!
      Nothing's gonna stop me—just watch me!

Optimism? Yes! Positive outlook? Yes! Glass-half-full? Yes!
   Perseverance? Yes, with a capital P! Perseverance is a choice!
      Put perseverance in your pocket and choose to use it!

Probably Not Perfect

Yup. That's me. Probably not perfect!

There was a time when I strove for perfection—
   in sports for elite competition—
      in academia for entry into select scholastic studies—
         in ER nursing where, in life and death,
            every minute (MI-nyute) detail matters—
               and, in my housekeeping where
                  everything was in its place, and
                     there was a place for everything.

But the new me,
   the here-and-now-me,
      is somewhat evolved,
         somewhat imperfect.
            And that is okay!

I still have high standards—very high standards.
   I still set the bar quite high.
      But, *not in search of the elusive perfection!*
         Uh-Uh. Nope. Not me.

I've come to realize
   that the pursuit of perfection in everyday living
      is both unrealistic and unattainable,
         and it is a totally unhealthy
            and an unreasonable approach and mindset.

The very minute I stopped trying
  to please others,
    or, to compare myself in attempt
      to match everyone else's perfecting standards
        or, to be better than what-is-simply
          capable-competent-worthy little ol' me—
            I was freed!
              The loads lifted!
                The pressure was off!

Sunlight filtered through all of the massive dark clouds of perfection,
  and the welcomed breeze of worthiness blew those clouds away!
    Away!!!

I *was* good enough, smart enough, able enough,
  ready enough, experienced enough, etc., etc..
    I could simply be, unapologetically, ME!
      I am enough! Imperfectly me, yet still, enough!

I have stopped chasing perfect.
  I am very happy now to evolve, to become,
    to better myself and to improve myself—to be—
      in a life *not* driven by best,
        or by first, or by Number 1, or by 'perfect'.

Here and now, in the moment,
  I'm happy to be me—
    Probably imperfect Wholehearted Me. Selah

Prayer Life

Dear God of all life and being, please hear my prayer.

I am fortunate to be able to say, that I have a healthy prayer life.
  I have learned over the years that my relationship with you
    is deepened, broadened, heightened,
      and made so very real, through prayer.

Our relationship is secure, strong, enduring,
  and it is built on a solid matrix of
    trust, faith, honesty, grace, and unconditional love.
      And yet, it is fluid, flowing, morphing,
        in the moment, in the now.

Our relationship is centering, grounding, forming.
  I am ever evolving in a really good way,
    through our prayer life together.

Our connecting and reconnecting,
  mostly through one-sided conversations from me,
    happens regularly, spontaneously, Wholeheartedly, and freely.

And, I give you thanks for hearing, and for listening,
  and, for being here for me in my wholesome prayer life. Amen.

Questions

The new 2022 United Church of Canada Call,
   calls each one of us into
      Deep Spirituality, Bold Discipleship, and Daring Justice.
         These are compelling and visionary words
            for a church in changing times.

I am born into and raised in the United Church of Canada.
   My ancestral heritage is Scottish and English,
      and I am drawn to the tenets of the ancient Celtic Wisdom.

I consider myself to be a modern day Celtic Christian.
   My faith is clearly a unique blend
      of the ancient Celtic Wisdom
         and modern Christian Insights.
            And I am totally comfortable with this.

The United Church invites its members to think for themselves,
   to open their minds in the realm of Christian teachings,
      to express their faith openly and freely,
         and to ask questions to clarify
            and seek relevance in modern times.

And I love this freedom to question, freedom to express,
    freedom to voice, freedom to challenge.
    The United Church has made bold steps forward
        in this last century, dealing with ultra-sensitive matters of
            inclusivity, human rights, and truth and reconciliation.

For me, being able to speak freely, ask questions, and express myself,
    in church, in my community, in the wider church community—
        all of this is a gift to me.

My wish is that in all denominations, and in all faith communities,
    people felt the freedom that I do,
        to contemplate, to ponder, to formulate questions,
            and to voice their words—openly, freely, respectfully—
            and that their questions and queries
                were heard, listened to, and answered.

This is a very big wish, a very big ask.
    Perhaps then someday,
        we can all be comfortable with asking the deeper questions
            that lay upon our hearts. May it be so.

Quiescence

It sounds rather lofty, but in reality, it is not.
    The name of my quiet subdivision here in Barrie, Ontario,
        is *Winding Woods Estates.*
            The woods themselves are truly winding,
                but the word estates is a misnomer, for sure!

Our neighborhood is made up of all two-storey homes
    which are cozy brick and vinyl-siding structures,
        nestled comfortably on a steep south-facing hillside,
            in a mixed coniferous-deciduous forest.
                Some lots run 150' deep into the quiet woods.

Q

Some of the tallest pines are more than 200 years old.
    There are beautiful birch groves, singleton crimson maple trees,
        and towering oak trees everywhere,
            casting their dappled shadows on the forest bed
                at mid-day, in all seasons.

In the evenings, in the setting sun,
    long long shadows are cast by golden horizontal light rays.
        It is almost ethereal—breath-taking indeed.

My husband prefers the backyard hammock—
    a brightly colored woven Nicaraguan treasure!

My favorite chair in the backyard is a giant basket chair,
    suspended from a sturdy chain on a gently arcing tall steel frame.
        Canvas-covered deep cushions make for comfortable seating.
            A canvas-covered gliding ottoman supports my legs and feet.

This chair is where I can drift, and dream,
    and muse and contemplate, and ponder and wonder and imagine—
    and read and learn, discover and discern,
        literally suspended—in thought, in time, in the woods.

This is my place of prayer.
    This is my special place. My Sanctuary. My haven. My retreat.
        I can while away the hours attuning, attending, communing.
            It is here that I found the reality of a deeply contemplative sit!
            All of my published books were born, right here!

My gardens are somewhat idyllic and wholly natural.
    They are not organized in color groups of flowers,
        nor are they arranged by order of height or genus of species.

My gardens are truly woodland gardens.
    Different and unusual shaped gardens are laid out
        using the steep lay of the land and towering trees as a matrix.
            A whimsical pine needle path emerges,
                as you stroll slowly past irregularly shaped garden beds.

Logs and thick branches, lay where they have fallen
  And giant rocks rest in their own places—where they've always been.
    Tall ornamental grasses grow where they will
      in the well drained sandy soil.
        Ivies and vines meander—cling and grasp and trail—
          they find their own place.

There is a central feature in every garden.
  A massive driftwood tree root.
    A stone-sculpted St Francis by the fountain in the pond.
      A rustic grey-washed trellis. A woodpile mantled with fungi.
        A four-foot tall statuary, which I have named Lady Peace.
          An old wooden lichen-encrusted parson bench
            and a rugged weather-beaten Muskoka chair.

My 'woodland garden dreamscape rising' simply fills me up—
  it feeds my soul, nurtures my spirit, and brings me to places—
    spacious and expansive places—that form me and heal me.

I crave my time in stillness.
  I look forward to the times when I can curl up,
    and empty my mind, empty myself of busy-ness
      and details and to-do lists and priorities—
        and housework!

When I intentionally clear my agenda, my afternoon or my weekend,
  with the intent of coming to stillness and simply taking care of me—
    practicing self-care is the current terminology—
      I begin to relax. Unwind. Let go.

I feel a certain release of worldly pressures.
  I feel a sense of peace slowly easing its way through my pores,
    and into my depths.
      All is well.

Q

And into the stillness I go,
   first in prayer, then in silence,
      then perhaps a little meditative time—
         or passive forest-bathing—Spring, Summer, Autumn.
            Winter is a tad chilly!

And in the stillness I remain.
   Sometimes I let a thought or two wander into my quietness,
      but then I just let those invasive thoughts drift away. Gone.

And still, in the stillness, I remain.

I listen. I hope for a nudge, or a word, an inner voice stirring,
   a still small voice,
      a beckoning, a voiceless voice that compels,
         or encourages, or steers, or affirms . . . .
            Sigh . . . .
               listening is such an interesting time!

And the longer I am still,
   the more I realize the restorative and healing powers of stillness.
      I feel more calm. I feel both rested, and, rejuvenated.
         I regain some strength
            even to the point of feeling energized!

It is as though my time of quiescence has quietly kick-started me.
   Stillness led to quiet led to calm led to peace led to quiescence.

(The structure of this last phrase just reminded me
   of the passage in Romans 5: 3–4
      where one good thing led to another, and to another,
         logically, progressively, seamlessly!)

In my woodland garden, in my Sanctuary, in the moment,
   let me be still.
      Let me enter the quiet.
         Let me quiesce.
            Sigh . . . .

Quaking Quavering Quivering—Not Me

Dear God, hear my prayer.

Fear can be overwhelming and downright paralyzing.
   But when I choose to stand tall and stand strong,
      trusting myself and trusting in you,
         there is nothing I cannot do.
           And I hear you ask of me . . . .

"Why all of the quaking, quavering and quivering? Stop!
Janis, my child, you've got this!"

And I settle. And my calm returns.
   And peace settles over me once again.
      And I say, thanks be to you, God.
         for strengthening me,
           for encouraging me,
              for believing in me,
                 for being with me,
                    again. Amen.

Resourcefulness—Reaching Outward, Inward, Upward

It's about knowing where to go, or knowing where to turn,
   when we need help.

When we are presented with an obstacle,
   an unusual or unprecedented situation, or the unknown,
     we can plough through and get 'er done,
       because we know we can—"Been there. Done that. Copy that."
        Or, we stop right there in our tracks
         and realize that we need help.
          This right here, is the moment of this passage.

We turn outward, to friends, family, neighbors,
   colleagues, ministers, teachers, and trained professionals,
     when we know we cannot do something
       or navigate something by ourselves.
        This is good. This is all good.

It's called being resourceful—
   it means having connections and relationships-in-place,
     which help to keep us moving forward,
       no matter what life brings our way.

We turn inward, to ourselves. We introspect.
   We know ourselves well—we know our strengths and weaknesses.
      And when we turn inward,
         we are seeking within ourselves to find a way
            to find an answer, to find the missing link
               or the important piece of the puzzle.

We dig deep and use our knowledge to piece things together,
   to figure it out, calculate it, or make an educated guess.
      And oftentimes, the answer is right there, right in front of our noses.
         We just needed to stop and think and believe in ourselves
            and be confident that we could work it out,
               figure it out, and make a go of it.

This again is being resourceful,
   and having the true grit to find it within ourselves to succeed.

And, sometimes, we turn inward for the wrong reason.
   Perhaps something is really personal, or demeaning,
      or embarrassing, even shameful.
         We do take steps to protect our pride
            and we keep it to ourselves.

"No one needs to know but me" we say.
   But we soon realize that it is bigger than we are
      and we won't be able to manage it own our own.

So, those who have a good relationship with God, they turn to God.
   They turn upward, looking upward,
      ever hopeful that God of all life and living
         will hear their prayer, and answer.

And this brings them comfort and solace,
   knowing that their burden is now shared.
      They are not in this alone.

And then there are those
  who do not have a relationship of any kind with God.
    And they are fearful of asking for God's help. So they don't.
      They feel they'll be judged by God,
        or worse,
          they'll be put to some test
            to measure their worthiness.
              Ouch!

We are all faced with situations, where we need help.
  We come to know ourselves over time, and our needs,
    and we surround ourselves with
      a network, a matrix, a community of people
        who are ready, willing and able,
          to help us when we ask.

This connecting—this being part of community—
  lays the groundwork for our future resourcefulness.
    Reaching inward, outward, upward,
      keeps us moving forward, toward, onward.

It keeps us in relationship—connected and interconnected.
  It keeps us strong and steady in our daily living.
    And this is good. This is all very good.

Resilience

In the face of adversity, at the point of plight, in the moment of might,
  I stand tall, I rise up and say
    "Away, away, be gone! Be done!"
      Not here! Not now! Not anyhow!"

And then my inner childlike voice speaks to me, quoting
  "I lift my eyes to the hills—
    from where will my help come?"[1]

---

1. NRSV Ps 121: 1

And of course, I do know the answer to this, and I call out strong,
  as sure as the rising and the setting of the sun,
    "God will help me. God will get me through."

And with this, I stand strong. Enlivened. Empowered.
  Resilient and ready to stand my ground.
    Resilient and strong to move forward, with God being my helper.

Can you feel, my resilience in my own written words?
  Does my hardiness, conviction
    and bounce-back-ability stir you?

Can you feel my steadfastness and my stick-to-it-ness?
  Can you feel my optimism and my drive
    contributing to my resilience?
      Do you feel it too?
        Do you want this too, for you—for Wholehearted You?

Release—Let Go—Let it Go

Dear God please hear my plea, hear my petition, hear my prayer.

Please help me to release my loads, and all that weighs me down.
  Help me to find the way,
    find my way, away from the burdens,
      the trials, the loads, the loads of care.

Help me to find strength and courage, and the endurance,
  to stay my course,
    to move forward unencumbered,
      to stand tall and strong once again.

Releasing is not easy. It is damn hard. I just need to let it go.
  I've tried and I'm still trying.
    When I release, when I let go, I'll be free.
      When I release, when I let it go, I'll feel like me, again.
        Help me God, release, let go, let it go . . . . Amen.

Sacred Sage of the Soul

Within our depths,
   within our own interior depths,
     there is wisdom,
       there is intuition—
         there dwells our Sacred soul within.

Often and increasingly,
   we need to slow down, pause, stop, and turn inward.
     We need to turn deeply inward
       to the great well of wisdom in our depths.
         We need to acknowledge that this wisdom
           is the wisdom of the ages
              which flows through eternity
                 like a river running through us.

Our ancestors carried this wisdom.
   They knew the Sacredness of their soul.
     They knew the inherent wisdom of the ages,
       and they knew to attune
         to the Sacred sage of their soul
           when met with challenging times.

Stop and take time.
  Go deep.
    Enter the deepest well, the Sacred well of your soul.
      Meet the Sacred sage and hearken, listen, attend.
        Honor the wisdom,
          of the Sacred sage of your soul.

Shimmerings

I talk about the Holy Lovelight in my life.
  I've written hymns, songs, poems, prayers,
    liturgies and whole Sunday services
      on the wonders of, and the essence of,
        the meaning of, and the blessings of,
          the Holy Lovelight of God.

My Lovelight prose is found in all three of my published books,
  Random and Nebulous—Nuancing the Psalms,
    and in *Light Beyond the River—Encountering the Sacred,*
    and in *My Indulgent Interior Life—Seasons of the Deep.*

"The Holy Lovelight is my own poetic waxing—
  my intricately laced and laden, chosen mystical word,
    for all of the gracious gifts given to me by God—
      love, joy, hope, peace, grace, wisdom, insight,
        strength, courage, encouragement,
          comfort, healing—presence—and so much more—
            all wrapped up in one exquisite word . . . .

Lovelight.
  It's a Showing,
    a Shining,
      a Shimmering,
        a Presence,
          a veritable Theophany!"[1]

---

1. [1] Excerpts from Janis Constable, *Random and Nebulous—Nuancing the Psalms,* 2021, page 6

S

I sense it. I feel it. I know of its powers.
   I intuit its meaning and its relevance in my daily living.
      I am honored by its very presence.
         It is gift. It is blessing.
            It is God present to me,
               in my midst, in my being, in my heart,
                  and deep deep down in my soul.

God's Holy Lovelight comes to me as a shimmering,
   something that is so very difficult for me, the poet,
      to even put into words.

God is Light,
   and I experience God's Light, God's Holy Lovelight, daily in my life.

The shimmering is welcomed, wanted, warming.
   This shimmering is tangible, palpable, real.
      This shimmering calls to me,
         makes its sparklescence known to me,
            and touches my soul.
               Sigh, I am so very blessed, indeed!

Seeking, Yet Sought

Dear God of Holy Lovelight, hear my prayer.

I am the seeker, yet, I am the sought.
   I know that you seek me out
      in the curves and the curls and the corners of my life.

You come to me as Light. You stir me with your Light.
   You comfort me and you lead me, in your Light.

You know that I seek you daily, moment by moment,
   for truly, you know my heart.
      You are Light and you dwell in me,
         and by this, I am known, loved, and understood.

I am sought and found.
   I am beloved, blessed, and called.
      It feels good to be sought by you.
         And humbly, I give you thanks. Amen.

Tough Enough

I don't want to be known as tough.
   Or headstrong. Or a warrior. Or a Titan.
      I don't need power, or authority or dominion, or territory—
         or a following.

But I do need to be tough enough.
   I need to know when to rise up strong to use my voice,
      to advocate for the weak and the frail
         and for those facing injustice(s).

I need to be tough enough to ensure
   that my needs and my family's and my community's needs are met,
      that I am not a doormat to be walked upon or stomped upon.

I need to be tough enough to stand my own ground
   when it is obviously the harder way to go.

I need to be tough enough
   to put my faith out in front of me
      and to let it guide me
         when I'm amongst those who have no faith.

I need to be tough enough to speak up for our blessed earth,
   whose voice—whose plaintive cries—
      have been unheeded and seemingly lost in the wilderness—
         whose needs grow stronger every day—
            urgently, fervently, overtly.

And I guess this all boils down to one thing. Grace.
   I need the grace to know
      the whens and the wheres and the for whoms
         to put on my overcoat of toughness.

I need to still be who I am—
   calm, gracious, diplomatic, willful and strong in my faith,
      kindhearted, warmhearted and wholehearted—
         yet, tough enough.

God grant me the grace to know when I need to be, tough enough.

Truth

Scholars, philosophers, researchers and theologians write about truth.
   So, I will not re-invent the wheel here.
      My wish is for you, in this moment,
         to feel the power—the magnetic power and pull—
            the strength and the draw of truth, through my words.

Think upon a time when you felt certain, absolutely certain.
   Think about something that to you, is factual.
      Examine these words—reality, correctness, authenticity, real.
         Even these words—accurate and right.

When truth is known, when truth is told, when truth is upheld,
   we have a gut sense, a gut reaction,
      a deep visceral knowing, and an affirmation of that truth.
         We intuit that truth.

It is this internal reaction,
  this moment, this knowing, this intuition arising,
    to which I am speaking.

Enter into your depths now, with a truth that is known to you.
  Is there a possibility that your truth is untruth?
    Is there a possibility that there are more possible truths?

Is there a chance that beyond your truth,
  there is new emerging truth that will shake your truth,
    shake your reality, or at least alter your reality somewhat?

How do you feel right now?
  How does it feel to have a core truth questioned, challenged,
    denied, devalued or even dismissed,
      pushed aside, refuted, stomped on or even tromped on?

Hard questions for sure.
  Pithy, profound, and uncomfortable questions for sure.
    It is hard to stay with this question.

These questions cannot be answered in a minute.
  They are worthy of our time, our attention, and our reflection.

Once we open ourselves to the truth, new truth, emerging truth,
  and cultural variations in understanding of truth,
    we can rest again, and feel grounded and secure.
      We can comfortably re-vision and reaffirm truth.
        Let us quest, and rest, in truth.

Tenacity—This

Dear God-with-me, please hear my prayer.

I do not want to be a ferocious lion, or a conquering hunting hawk.
  But I do need tenacity for the journey. This.

On my journey into Wholehearted Living,
   I need to hold fast to values, wisdom and faith—
     and my integrity.

Please help me maintain my gracious approach,
   my gentle spirit, and my compassionate heart,
     all the while helping me to grow in tenacity. This.
     There's a balance and I need to find it.

With you God, as my helper, all things are possible.
   Nothing is impossible with you.
     I feel my own tenacity arising in these very words.
     And this is good. Amen.

Uniqueness

Look out your window into the world.
    The world is full of uniqueness.
        People, places, things.
           Color, texture, depths.
                Education, arts and culture.
                    Social, political, religious.
                Rural, urban, rurban.

And now, simply look inward.
    Introspect. Contemplate. Ponder.
        Look at your own uniqueness!

What is it? What defines it?
    What makes you, unique? What makes you, you?
        Is uniqueness fluid, dynamic, alive,
            or stationary, stuck and final?
                Sit with these questions awhile,
                    and enjoy where it takes you!

In this moment, you are unique. And in the next, and in the next.
    Uniqueness is a quality, an essence of individuality.

Wholehearted Me A–Z!

One of a kind, special, solitary, unusual, and remarkable—all are close.
But, unique is truly unique. There is no other word for it, but unique.

Consider now three realms—three words—*'Time, Place and Person.'*

Every moment, is a unique moment in *time*.
 There are no two moments alike, never-ever-ever!
  Time itself is unique onto itself.
   There is nothing in this world that is like *time*,
    or a close cousin of *time*, or a nuance of *time*.
     Time itself is unique.

Place, and space, and spaciousness and spatiality are all unique.
 Simply unique.

And every *person*, every human being is unique.
 Our DNA proves it. Personality shows it. Mirrors reflect it.
  If it's not unique, it is different.
   You are uniqueness all wrapped up in one-of-a-kind-you!

In all three realms,
 in *'Person, Place and Time'*,
  uniqueness reigns. Period.

So, where is all of this going?
 Let us celebrate our uniqueness!
  Truly come to see, know and understand
   our individuality and our differences!
    We are all the same, only in that we are all unique.

In your own self-examen, in your journey into Wholehearted Living,
 in your daily affirmations,
  celebrate your uniqueness
   and feel grounded in your own uniqueness.
    Arise in the wonder of your uniqueness!
     Do not fear it—celebrate it!
      Wholeheartedly!

U

Let your uniqueness shine for all the world to see.
   Be yourself. Love yourself. Love being you!
      Simply, uniquely, be you!

Unbridled Mindset—Unbridled Me!

Sigh. No chains. No limits or boundaries.
   No brick walls. No impasses.
      No black holes or sinkholes.
         No rules. No restrictive carved-in-stone-doctrine or law.

The sky is the limit—NO WAIT! The sky is NOT the limit—
   for visioning, creativity, self-expression,
      for thinking outside the box, coloring outside the lines,
         for love and joy and hope and peace and grace—and faith.

This is me. This is my moment. This is my place and my time.
   Unleashed. Unbridled. Free.
      Unbridled me. Sigh . . . . Wheeeeeeeee . . . . !!!

Unconditional Love

Dear God of all love and loving, hear my prayer.

Unconditional is much like the concept of *unbridled*.
   It is boundless and unlimited.
      It is ever-present and free flowing.
         It is not reserved or withheld or rationed.
            It is not attached with strings,
               and it has no qualifiers.

Unconditional love is your love, God.
   It is motherly, fatherly, sisterly, brotherly, neighborly.
      As Light is seen as a spectrum of colors,
         so too, your Light is spectrified.
            Like a prism. Like a rainbow of many colors.

And I am grateful to know this love, firsthand, and to receive this love,
   in all of its colors, in all of its glory, in all of its shimmering Light!
      In my journey into Wholehearted Living,
         I vow to be this love, for all who need.

Help me God,
   to be this love,
      to be love,
         to be unconditional love. Amen.

Validation through Voices, Vibrance, and Vitreous Lustre

Voices. When I hear voices calling, I stop. I listen. I instinctively listen.
   This is not a psychotic break, nor is it a schizophrenia episode.
     This is me, attuning to the voices that speak to me.

The voice of my own creativity and my desires.
   The voice of my dreams.

The voice of reality, and of the here and now.
   The voice of morality and conscience, and of authority and discipline.
     The voice of reason and wisdom.
        The voice of the sage soul deep within.

The voice of experience and yesterday.
   The voice of my Celtic ancestors.
     The visionary voice of tomorrow.
       The voice of Abba.
          The still small voice.
            The voiceless voice of God.

How do I know? How do I discern? How do I differentiate?
   I just know. It's all a mystery, and that's just fine with me.

These voices are real.
  They ground me, guide me,
    protect me, and help me in my journey.
      It's my job, my duty to respect these voices
        and to discern their priority
          and their relevance and their meaning
            in my life, in the moment,
              and in my here and now.

Is there any teaching in this?
  Is there something special in this that I need to share?
    Perhaps these words will be affirming words for you.
    Perhaps you'll acknowledge that you too, listen—
      that you too listen and honor many, many voices.

And maybe, just maybe, you'll feel validated, and valued,
  knowing that you are instinctively listening
    and relying on those same powerful voices.

And hopefully, next time the voices call out to you,
  you'll smile inwardly, knowingly, gratefully.
    Let all of the voices be heard.

Vibrance . . . . is such a lovely word—
  Colors of the soul arise!
    Vibrance . . . . is seen and felt and heard—
      And surely what I need to thrive!

A Wholehearted person has vibrance!
  They are engaged, and energized,
    and they can simply light up a room with their energy!

V

Their energy is palpable.
   They are enlivened from the core.
      Their charisma—and their magnetism—is visible!
         They are grounded, sure and ready.
            They are compassionate and they serve with a Servant Heart.
               Their faith is strong and they live out their faith.

They aren't necessarily leaders, or dominant, or center-of-the-crowd.
   Even the introverts living the Wholehearted Life
      can be described as solid, engaging, stirring, compelling,
         and full of vibrance in their sure and quiet presence.

Is there someone in your life, that you know well,
   who is Wholehearted, who is living the Wholehearted Life?
      What does their vibrance look like, sound like, feel like?
         My friend Pat MacDonald comes to mind!
            Take time to reflect on their vibrance.
               Visualize it. Sense it. Value it.

Please don't spend this moment comparing yourself to others!
   That is not the intention!

Please take time to study what their vibrance looks like
   and then it is up to you to embody the qualities
      which will highlight or enhance your own vibrance.
         Have some fun with vibrance!

Vitreous Lustre—"having the glass-like lustre of a nonmetallic mineral"
   is the dictionary technical definition.

My softer, gentler, touchy-feely,
   evocative and highly spiritually-charged working definition
      of human holy vitreous lustre is . . . .

"the living Light that shines, that emanates,
   that arises from deep within the human being,
      from the human essence,
         from the depths of the human soul.
            Adulariant and reflective in the same breath."

My own poetic woolgatherings
   took me on an amazing lifelong journey into the Holy Lovelight—
      into the wondrous and ethereal lustre of Holy Lovelight—
         into a life of Living in the Light.

Arise. Shine. Shine your Light. Shine your living lustrous Light—
   Here and now and in all your days!

Let Voices, Vibrance and Vitreous Lustre—
   the sounds, the sights and the Lights—
      let ALL of these be yours as you journey inwards,
         seeking to know their parts, and their relevance
            in your very own Wholehearted Life.

Vocabulary Matters

These are my own personal ramblings and my wrestlings
   with important categorical words which have critically shaped my life—
      my Wholehearted Life

The following is a list of vocabulary, compiled for you,
   of words within which to find your place, find your place of comfort,
      find your place in the world, and find your place in time—
         vocabulary within which to find yourself, and define yourself.
            Take time and enter into the depths
               of these very very important and timeless words . . . .

Soul—the innermost essence of self, of virtue, of passion.
   Poetically put—an illuminating expression of innerness and inner-tude.
      Intimacy, connection, and Sacredness—
         all of these rise up and find their home in the realm of the soul.

V

Spirit—an energy or a vibe or a certain enlivened presence
  which is discernable, palpable, and shareable.
    Its dimensionality is questioned by many—defined by none.
      Along with its own power and timing, it has movement and flow.
      Its very inertia, is mystery. Selah

Spirituality—the deep and true connectedness
  and relational threads in all life and living.
    Body mind and spirit are nestled, nurtured,
      balanced and whole, in the realm of spirituality—
        in the wonders of spirituality.
          There is an inherent and evocable reverence therein.

Religion—a denominational organization based upon
  historical and/or traditional teachings, doctrines and creeds—
    centered on the Divine—centered on God.

Religion may be conservative, progressive and liberal,
    or evangelical in nature, in approach.
      Personal and communal rituals are practiced
        with both seasonal, weekly and daily regularity.

Reverence—an outward or inward feeling, gesture or display—
  a manifestation of one's genuine and deep respect, honor and worship
    of that/which/whom is deemed Holy/Sacred/Divine.

Holy/Sacred/Divine—noun, when prefaced by "the",
  or adjective, describing
    that/which/whom is reverenced,
      simply in its being Godly, of God, God.

Faith—both the spoken and unspoken credence and reverence,
  given by a person to themselves, to another, to a higher power.
    It is a commitment to and a conviction in
      that/which/whom is Holy, Sacred, Divine—in God.
        It may be described as deep, strong, unwavering and solid,
          or, as floundering, weak, contesting, or lost.
            Faith flows like an ever-flowing stream
              into the River of Life—into Eternity. Selah

Wholehearted Me A–Z!

Beliefs—strong positive and affirmative feelings
   toward principles, doctrine, and timeless wisdom,
      which are all based in truth and righteousness,
         serving both the individual and the greater good.

Morals—the very matrix of mindset, or, way of thinking and being,
   which an individual or community deem to be plainly wholesome—
      pure and right and good and true.

Affirmations—are "I-Me-Mine Statements", spoken or penned,
   which put one's whole self, whole person, whole being,
      in-perspective-in-the-moment-in-the-now.
         Affirmations shape, clarify and direct,
            both personhood and personal pathways.
               Affirmations are powerful sentiments of self—
                  of self-knowing.

Grace—warm and welcomed, yet truly, a nebulous entity.
   A verb and a noun.
      An action and a thing.
         A way and a gift—even a presence.
            A blessing bestowed, given and received freely.

May you grace others—may you choose to grace others.
   May you be graced by God.
      May you know in your heart, forever and always,
         the wonders and the powers of the grace of God.

Wisdom—Worldly wisdom and deep inner intuitive wisdom
   are more than simply knowledge, more than insight,
      more than understanding or comprehension.

Wisdom is at once a foundation, cornerstone and touchstone,
   and, a most coveted and motivating self-actualization pyramidal peak.

Wisdom, like love, boldly defies
   definition, description, boundaries, and limits.

V

Wisdom is solid and sure, and grounding,
 yet, it is truly evolving, fluid and responsive through time.
  Wisdom lives. Wisdom is alive.

Muse now on just this. What is wisdom?
 A quality? A state of being? An essence? A goal? An achievement?
  A spectrified noun with many and mysterious shades of grey?
   Is there truly an all-encompassing black and white
    definition of wisdom, out there?
     Has there ever been?

Take time and find your own words
 to paint your very own vision of wisdom.
  Put words to your knowing.
   Put words to your vision.
    Put words to your wisdom.
     Let wisdom become. Let wisdom be!

And then, after forming and feeling out your own words of Wisdom,
 spend time in the question "What is the real meaning in my heart,
  of Soul, Spirit, Spirituality, Religion,
   Reverence, Holy/Sacred/Divine,
    Faith, Belief, Morals, Affirmations, and Grace?"

I love words!
 I love contemplating the depth of meaning of our words.
  Words and their meanings are powerful. So powerful.
   They are grounding, centering, and potentially directive.
    The more we are comfortable with the words we use every day,
     the more we are confident and ready
      to immerse ourselves in the colors of living,
       in the curves and corners and chaos of life,
        in the comfort and clarity
         of Wholehearted Living.

Vision

Dear God, hear my prayer.

I have a vision, a growing vision of Wholehearted Living,
   and what it means to live a Wholehearted Life.

I have a vision of myself
   emerging as a Wholehearted being.
     I have a vision of embodying Wholeheartedness, that in so doing,
       others may come to see and feel—that they may be moved—
         to step into the Wholehearted Life.

I have some work yet to do. Some good work to do!
   I need to do more soul searching, some more contemplating,
     and some much needed interior work
       in order to fully grasp the concepts and the images.

And, I need to continue to pray over wholeheartedness.
   I believe it is something that you God, are well acquainted with,
     and something that you would uphold and value.

I will continue to study, explore, and try out my wings, with your help.
   You and I, we will walk this journey together,
     hand in hand, heart in heart, together as One.
       May this vision become reality—
         with your help, I pray. Amen.

Wholehearted Me—Brenda's Light

I am choosing to share this vignette,
    as allegory—as story with a much deeper meaning—
        as story imbedded with the truths of Wholehearted Living.

May you feel my positivity and my positive outlook.
    Glass-half-full living is highlighted, as is *joie de vivre*.

May you see and feel the depth
    of my engaged living, of our engaged living.

May you take to heart the sensitivity, the compassion, the love,
    and the genuineness of my words.

May you note the honor and respect
    and the trust within the relationships.

May you see the harmony
    and then feel when the harmony slips away.

    Self-awareness and self-affirmation, confidence, self-worthiness,
        connectedness and belonging are interlaced throughout.

The story of Brenda's Light is shared here,
  through the lens of Wholehearted Living.
    May you, like Brenda, come to embody
      the core truths of Wholehearted Living,
        in every day, in every moment, in every breath.

Brenda was Light. Brenda was hope.
  Brenda, was glass-half-full-living,
    and personal positivity, and global optimism,
      all wrapped up in one human package, called 'My Sister'.

But, Brenda's world was dark.
  She was the firstborn.
    In 1956, our maritime-farmer-father,
      and Toronto-born-city-girl-mother,
        were absolutely delighted with the news
          of finally conceiving—of finally having a baby!

Mom labored a really long time, 36 hours,
  before the doctor decided on a C-Section.
    There were some questions after birth,
      about prolonged oxygen deprivation,
        and possible fetal distress.
          Only time would tell, down the road,
            about any deficits, or delays,
              or disabilities.

Brenda grew up happy, lighthearted, and really good-natured.
  She was always smiling.
    However, she was painfully shy among adults and children alike, and,
      more often than not, she would fall behind in school,
        especially in the basics—reading, writing and arithmetic.

Dad was always pitching in—he made time every night
  to give Brenda extra help with her reading and math homework.
    He also took lots of extra time
      on the weekends to play with her.

He made sure she could catch a ball,
  even though she struggled a lot with her eye-hand co-ordination.
    He taught her to always keep her eye on the ball.

She struggled even, to ride her bike—her balance was very poor.
  He was still running beside his little girl on the bike,
    long after I, two years younger, learned to ride by myself.
      That didn't matter.
        What did matter, is that he was always helping her,
          and she gladly accepted his help. Always.

Whatever extra help she needed, Dad was there.
  She needed him—and his help—so very much.
    He understood that she could succeed, with a little extra help.
    He truly believed in this, and, he believed in her.
      And, BJ grew up feeling the assurance, the support,
        and the encouragement of her doting, loving daddy.

In those days, in the 50's and 60's,
  kids weren't identified or labeled in school,
    with learning disabilities.
      They simply moved through the school system,
        at their own pace, with a lot of support from their families.

Brenda never, ever, failed a grade,
  and with my dad's help,
    she was able to stay with her own cohort,
      year after year after year.

At age 11, Brenda was diagnosed with diabetes.
   I was the younger sister, 9 years old,
      and I began to witness the turbulence in our family—the rocky road—
         the big and small burdens borne by the whole family,
            in the complexities of diabetes management.

And of course, Mom stopped baking pastries, cakes and cookies.
   There were no more chocolate treats or ice cream cones.
      We all ate more vegetables, less meat, tons of fruit,
         and gallons of milk. So much milk!

Mom took classes—classes for mothers of new diabetics—
   to learn all about diabetes management, and insulin,
      and the old fashioned urine testing for sugar levels.
         Brenda's life became regimented. Managed. Micro-managed.
            Controlled. Measured. Restricted. Limited.

Everyone was so fearful of the dreaded low blood sugar episodes.
   Corn-syrup-by-the-tablespoon-by-mouth,
      was the quickest and safest fix.
         The corn syrup would almost instantly pull her back
            from the brink of delirium and incoherence,
               back to full cognitive awareness.
                  And, it boosted her sagging blood sugar level
                     long enough in order to get some real,
                        carb-rich foods into her, safely.

Brenda was bullied at school,
   by kids who just didn't understand what diabetes was.
      All they knew was that she was not normal.
         Kids can be so mean. They were mean-spirited, to say the least.

But, you know, Brenda moved forward. Head held high.
   She remained painfully shy, but, she had a certain Light about her.
      Brenda's Light shone beautifully.
         She found joy in little things. Simple things.
            She laughed loudly at things she thought were funny.
               Her giggles and her laughter were infectious!

W

Anyone who knew Brenda, was drawn to her *joie de vivre*.
　She walked through life contented, safe, and sure.
　　She lived through darkness, with her deficits and her diabetes,
　　　but she did not let these d-words define her.

In her teenage years, she was not much of an athlete,
　so, she turned to good books, and reading teen magazines.

More of a loner, or a one-on-one-kind-of-a-friend,
　she avoided social groups and parties,
　　and places where she felt awkward.

She was happy at home.
　She was happiest at home.
　　She could be herself at home.
　　　She was hopeful at home.

At 18, she was accepted into university, to study sociology and psychology,
　and Brenda loved what she studied.
　　It grounded her. It well-rounded her.

It opened her whole self to knowledge,
　wisdom and colorful insights of the human condition.
　　She already had an inborn understanding of humanity.
　　　She saw the Light in others,
　　　　and she understood the powers of their darkness.

She had a really big heart.
　It was laced with caring and compassion and conviction.
　　She felt connected to the underdogs,
　　　the misunderstood, and the forgotten.

She believed there was hope for everyone.
　She knew personally what it felt like to be helped out along the way,
　　to be encouraged, to be pointed in the right direction.
　　　She knew what it felt like to live in hope—
　　　　to always look outward and see in front of her,
　　　　　a glass half full.

Needless to say, more darkness lurked for BJ.
  It would soon befall her path.
    In her 3rd year of university, she had to drop out of school,
      due to some alarming symptoms.

One whole year later, she was finally diagnosed with Addison's disease.
  She would have to take oral steroids for the rest of her life
    to control her symptoms.

Note to all. Steroids and insulin together is like a really bad marriage.
  They are never meant to be taken together, long term.
    Steroids play extreme havoc with blood sugar levels.

The doctor's predicted, that with the rollercoaster highs and lows
  of blood sugars over the long term,
    that Brenda would likely not see her 40th birthday.

Well, that was one hard prognosis to ponder.
  It was like she had been sentenced to death.
    A slow, unpredictably predictable death-walk.

Mom and Dad did all they could
  to support her through this terrible news,
    but their own hearts were breaking.
      Their little girl's life would be a short one.

They became different people.
  They were secretly angry, with very, very, very short fuses.
    Cranky pants. Anxious. They felt lost. Disconnected.
      They lost their natural joy of life.
        They were stressed.
          Stressed to the max
            with their anticipatory grieving.

But Brenda. My goodness! She took all of this in stride!
  She could see that our parents were falling apart.
    She intuitively sensed that SHE was the source
      of their angst, and their grief, and their pain.

She summoned everything she could to help them—
   to be there for them—
      to make sure that they could still 'be living'
         while she was slowly dying.

She was the glue that kept the family
   laughing together, sharing life together, and moving onward,
      making the most of—the best of—a difficult situation.

I remember when she bought
   a hand-painted iron fry pan, at an arts and crafts sale.
      Painted on the bottom of the pan were the words
         "Happiness is Homemade".

She knew in her heart, she intuited,
   that true happiness comes from within, and that indeed,
      no one could make you happy, but you.
         I learned so much about humanity and about hope,
            through my sister, Brenda.

Brenda was hope. Brenda was Light.
   Her world was dark.
      Her physical and medical struggles were dark,
         but she herself, was Light.

Brenda was determined to live out the rest of her days,
   in happiness and in hope—and with as much independence as possible.
      At age 31, she finally got her driver's license!

She immediately flew home to Nova Scotia, by herself,
   to stay with cousins and friends of the family.
      She was there for a whole month.

She rented a car and went for many day-long drives
   up and down the old shoreline roads of Nova Scotia,
      and she zigzagged across the rolling, sloping,
         agricultural lands, inland.

On those old dusty country backroads and sideroads,
　　she was experiencing a sense of freedom like she'd never, ever known.
　　　　She was declaring her independence and her rights to joyful living.
　　　　　　She invented joyriding!

She got lost a few times.
　　Most certainly she struggled with reading maps—
　　　　but she'd always stop and ask a farmer along the way,
　　　　　　who then so kindly,
　　　　　　　　helped her to get to where she wanted to go.

She found joy in the moment, happiness in just being,
　　and she found hope around every curve, around every corner.

At age 35, every imaginable side effect
　　of long-term poorly managed blood sugars, caught up with her.

She went totally blind.
　　She lost all sensation in both of her hands
　　　　and in all of her fingers,
　　　　　　and she simply could not grip anything.

Her distal circulation failed
　　and her right toe amputation was followed
　　　　by a below the knee amputation,
　　　　　　and later, above the knee.

Then, at age 38, her kidneys gave up the ghost,
　　and she was in irreversible acute renal failure.

The night before she died in hospital,
　　she SHARED her words of wisdom,
　　　　she TOLD funny stories of 'remember when',
　　　　　　and she SHOWED her love to her family.
　　　　　　　　She KNEW her time was near, yet,

SHE was filling US with hope.
   SHE was showing US by her example, what hope looked like.
   SHE was leading US on a path of hope.

On Thanksgiving in 1994, she died ever so peacefully,
   in a private room at St Joseph's Hospital in Toronto,
      overlooking the calm, still waters of Lake Ontario,
         at sunset.

She lived as Light. She died as Light. She, to this day, is Light.

If there are any takeaways from this story, let it be these words . . . .

We can choose to dwell in darkness, or we can walk in the Light.
   We can choose to be sad, or, we can choose to be happy.
      We need to look for joy *everywhere, in everything, all the time*.
         We need to see the glass of life, as half-full.
         And then, we need to count our blessings.

We CAN live the Wholehearted Life.
   We CAN live with a heart of gratitude.
      We CAN live with hearts full of hope.
         We CAN live in the Light.
            We can BE Hope. We can BE Light. Amen!

Wildness

We've all heard similar expressions . . . .
   'Take a walk on the wild side.'
      'Release the beast.'
         'Unleash the untamed in you.'
            'Discover the primal, tribal, WILDNESS of YOU!'

Sounds a little frightening, I'm sure!
  We choose to, and we do find comfort in,
    living our lives with as much order and safety as we can.
      Chaos is avoided, even frowned upon.
        And, as a routine way of living, chaos is truly undesirable.

Order is our comfort zone.
  Boundaries and rules demarcate our comfort zones.
    Law and order give us structure, and peace.

But somewhere deep inside of us,
  is the enlivened primitive soul.
    The protector of family. The provider. The nurturing spirit.
      The uncaged, untamed freedom-seeking explorer
        of the uncharted waters,
          and the conquest-seeking hunter and gatherer.
            The inquisitive creative genius
              that builds things, adapts things
                and fixes things.

And, the adventurer, seeking new thrills and delights!

Were we to tap into our own primitiveness, we might be frightened.
  We might feel lost without our rules and our guidelines.

We might feel unsafe in a place, in a space,
  where territory is continually challenged,
    where there are predators lurking.

We might not be able to sleep, or even rest,
  for fear of the unknowns, and the unseens.

I'M NOT asking anyone to try anything
  where they will feel unsafe, or vulnerable, or unprotected.
    Not at all!

I AM asking you to visualize
   what wildness of thought, wildness of emotion,
     wildness of creativity, wildness of self-expression,
       wildness of dreaming, wildness of visioning,
         looks like and feels like for you!

Again, this cannot be answered in a minute.
   It IS a contemplative reach, a stretch.
     It IS an intentional wandering out of the comfort zone
       into the possibility of uncomfortable thinking.
         We don't go there easily. We just don't!
           Please, please, please just give it a try!

Wildness of spirit, wildness in creativity, wildness of self-expression
   are all things that we experienced regularly as children.
     And life itself—adulting—has put a damper—
       it has thrown many dampers on this original wildness.

We CAN reclaim it! We CAN find it!
   We CAN intentionally search, practice,
     and experiment with our innate wildness!

Say something out loud that you've never said out loud before.
   Write a memoir and distribute it to friends and family.
     In it, write down the good stories, and the hard-to-tell stories.
       Sit down intentionally to read a genre that is
         completely outside of your comfort zone—
           That for me would be Futuristic Sci-Fi!

Have a heart-to-heart with a trusted friend,
   and enter into a conversation about a sensitive matter.
     Not with the intention of shock factor, rather,
       with the intention of discovering
         something about yourselves in that conversation.
           Risk speaking out and being vulnerable.

Discover your innermost you—
   your suppressed subdued and hidden you—
     your wild and untamed you!

I'm giving you permission to drop your personal inhibitions
   and your filters—
      to step right out
         of that safe and cushioned place called comfort zone!
            Be wild! Don't be uncomfortable! Go nuts! Have fun!
               Find a new comfort zone in your wildness within!

Wisdom

Dear God, hear my prayer.

You, are wisdom.
   I intuit the wisdom of the ages flowing deep within my soul.
      The world turns and turns and the wisdom flows and flows,
         and all is well.

It is when I turn away from your wisdom,
   and when I tune out the wisdom arising in me,
      that I get into trouble.
         Usually deep deep trouble.

Please remind me to turn to your wisdom.
   Help me to tune into the wisdom of the ages in my very depths,
      that I may move forward, that I may rise up,
         that I may answer the call,
            with both you and wisdom befriending me. Amen.

X Marks the Spot

Pirates of olde tagged their primitive maps
   with an X marking the spot,
      naming the location of the buried or hidden treasure.

And this here, this is a modern day passage about our treasure!
   A passage about goals that we seek.
      A passage about what we hope to find.
         A passage about naming treasures.

'Shoot high, reach for the sky'—an old expression about goal setting
   inferring that we need to
      set big goals, dream big,
         and set our sights on distant but attainable targets.

In a world of moving forward,
   in the world of becoming,
      in the realm of seeking, to embody Wholeheartedness
         in its absolute fullness,
            we must first name the prize and treasure the prize.
            And Wholeheartedness, is indeed the prize.

We named it—Wholeheartedness—
   and for sure we are valuing it, upholding it, and treasuring it!
      We are reading and writing books about it!
         Of course we have named and treasured it.
            Step One done! Check!

Step Two is all about intention, and planning, and setting the bar.
   We know what we want in Wholeheartedness, and we learn more about
      what it looks like and feels like in our everyday living,
         through our reading, through our studies,
            and through our personal reflections.
               Here and now, this is a work in progress.
                  Step Two—Ongoing.

Step Three is all about Action. Taking action. Taking pro-active steps.
   It's time to take steps, measurable steps,
      and take action, toward Wholeheartedness.

Consider these for Step Three . . . .
   Be vibrant today. Let the world see and feel your enlivened spirit.
      Show compassion through a random act of kindness today.
         Advocate for one who cannot speak for their own needs.
            Address a niggling problem in your relationship,
               and get to the heart of the matter
                  by having a conversation
                     and openly expressing your concerns.

Be vulnerable—show your vulnerability.
   Exude positivity today and affirm your self-worth.
      Talk to God in prayer and listen for guidance.
         Speak gratefully. Act gratefully. Be grateful.

Step Three—Ongoing. Step Three will always be ongoing
   on the journey into Wholehearted Living. And this is a good thing!

X

Step Four is all about reflecting.
  Looking back to note changes, goals achieved, treasures found,
    and deciding if the current treasure maps are accurate.
      Seeing if the actions in the journey meet all of the needs,
        and, relocating X's on the map
          for clarity, for ease, and for success.
            Step Four—is Perpetually ongoing!!!

Oh my! My soft toned and encouraging spiel
  has become yet another formatted checklist,
    another how-to, another protocol for success. Sorry!

I make X's! I mark the spot. I name my treasures, my goals!
  I guess it's just so easy for me to slip into a goal-setting way of life.
    If anything, return to Step Three, internalize it,
      and keep on adding suggestions—
        keep adding actions and do-ables that work for you
          in your daily quest,
            in your daily journey in Wholeheartedness.

Make it fun! Make it interesting. Affirm yourself along the way.
  I invite you to rise up to the challenge of Wholehearted Living,
    with an energized spirit and a growing desire for 'becoming'.
      Approach with a lust for all that is
        new and fresh and renewing
          for your whole person, body mind and spirit.
            Have fun!

Xyphoid

Xyphoid Process. Pronounced either ZIGH-foid, or, ZIFF-oid.
  The xyphoid process is a bone
    at the very end of the sternum,
      in the human being.
        It is protuberant in some,
          and barely palpable in others.

Its sole purpose is to provide a place of attachment—
  a strong unyielding attachment—
    for a large number of moving parts,
      mostly muscles, ligaments and bones.

What is it in you,
  that provides strength and attachment and stability for many parts,
    all moving in different directions
      with different priorities and purposes?

What is it in you that is steadfast and sure and dependable,
  and always there when you need it?

What is it in you that provides connection?

What is it in you that is core, central, upfront and center—yet innermost?

What is it in you that is so natural
  that its work is effortless, seamless, and barely perceptible?

What is it in you that you would have difficulty in living your life,
  if you suddenly had to live without it?

The answer my friend, is NOT blowing in the breeze.
  The answer is yours for the seeking. Seek and ye shall find!

"Xtraordinary"

Dear God who holds the mysteries of life and living, hear my prayer.

I must say dear God,
  that I have had one colorful life,
    that I have lived one colorful life!
      One extraordinary life for sure, with you by my side!

I have known you,
  and I have grown through you,
    and you have shown me the way.

X

And 'extraordinary' does not elevate me, or put me up on a pedestal.
   Not at all! Rather, it has energized me!
      It has given me a taste,
         a zest for the colors and depths and textures of life!
            I've been totally engaged and immersed in my life.
               'Extraordinary' has raised my spirit,
                  and given me vision for Wholehearted Living.
                  It has humbled me
                     and brought me to my knees.

God of life, God of Extraordinariness, God of the Extraordinary,
   Thank you! Amen!

Yesterday

'Yesterday' can stir up a multitude of emotions.
   Yesterday is made up of
      memories, sentiments, relationships, stages of life,
         beginnings, new beginnings, endings,
            dreams, dreams realized,
               dreams adrift, dreams lost.

There is a lot of weight in yesterday.
   Yesterday is the foundation of today—of me, today.
   Yesterday laid down the groundwork, the matrix,
      the infrastructure, the inner workings, of me.

I am a body mind and spirit.
   I have been formed,
      physically, mentally, emotionally, spiritually.
         I am complex, because yesterday was complex.

I need to fully understand my yesterday,
   in order to fully understand my today,
      and to make plans for my tomorrow.

Y

Yesterday is a library, a reference library, a resource center.
   Yesterday is alive with information, teeming with information
      that can be retrieved, reviewed,
         reassessed, and re-imagined.

Yesterday can be a starting point.
   In looking back, I get a reference point.
      I get a sense of place and space, and relevance in time.
         I get a perspective of my here and now,
            based on my 'back then'.

Yesterday is a cornerstone, an anchor, a solid footing,
   even a braided tether.
      It secures me, and it is unshakeable, and fast.
         Yesterday itself is fixed,
            and unchangeable.
               I don't know how to rewrite yesterday—
                  and I certainly don't need to!

Knowing all of this I feel strong. Very strong.
   I have had good things in my life, and bad.
      And, I have had hard things too,
         to deal with, to navigate,
            to comprehend, and to forgive.

I know to look to yesterday,
   to see where I've come from,
      to understand where I've come from,
         and how I've become who I am today.

I love my yesterday because it is part of me.
   It is a very large part of me.
      And it *will probably* be the largest part of me,
         seeing that I am 65 years young
            and there most surely won't be 65 more years of me
               in my future!!!

But, I will not dwell in yesterday.
  I am present here today.
    I cherish my roots, and my story,
      and I am still writing my story, here and now.

I value my yesterday.
  I celebrate my yesterday.
    And I am grateful for my yesterday.
      And I move forward, with energy, with hope,
        with optimism, with anticipation,
          knowing that I am grounded,
            knowing my faith is strong.
              I am solid, I am strong,
                because of yesterday.

I'm living here in the moment, here in my now, deeply engaged in life.
  And, I'm living with eyes to my future,
    whatever that may be,
      whatever that may look like for me.

And if that isn't Wholehearted Living . . . .
  then I had better read more literary works
    from Brené, and Koshin, and Rachel !!!

YOU-ology

This whole book has been a reflection.
  A study. A study of me and a study of you!
    We're all in this together!

We're all on this earth, us human beings,
  connected and interconnected in our communal and social ways.
    Things that are good for me, in a communal sense,
      are likely going to be good for you too.

Y

It's now your turn, to turn inward. To look at 'you'.
   No sense reading all of this stuff,
      unless you take some or all of it to heart,
         and do a personal exam, a daily self-examen.

It's your turn to introspect, to contemplate, to ponder YOU!
   This is YOU-ology !!!
      No egocentricity here. No sin in self-focused review.
      No shame in having a healthy interior life.
         Only rewards. Rewards for you to reap!

Enjoy your reflection of you.
   Enjoy your enlightenment in Wholeheartedness.
      Enjoy becoming.
         Enjoy finding yourself and re-imagining yourself!

You are a child of God, called to do good works here on earth.
   Big or small, your works will connect you to others.
      You are born with a Sacredness within,
         and an innate interconnectedness
            with all other Sacred life and living.

Study YOU! Know YOU! Love YOU! Celebrate YOU!
   God bless YOU in your YOU-ology course.
      God bless you in your journey into Wholehearted Living.
         May YOU move forward, being YOU, loving YOU!

Yearning

Dear God of all our hearts, please hear my prayer.

I pray that we will always have
   the want, the desire, the need, to yearn.

Yearning stirs us, lights us up from inside, calls us, and directs us.
  Yearning is Light.
    Yearning comes from within.
      May we listen to our yearnings,
        and act upon our yearnings,
          that we may become, that we may grow,
            that we may move forward in
              Wholehearted Living, at its very best. Amen.

Zeal and Zest

Zeal and Zest—simply the best!
   Feel it. Claim it. Embody it. Share it.
     Wholeheartedly!!!

Zirconias and Zinnias

Zirconias are synthetic, processed, human-made.
   Zinnias grow naturally, wild and free.

We are born of God, as our beginning,
   but we develop and grow
     as a product of our circumstance and our environment.

In time, we become partly 'self-made'.
   We are homegrown of our own individual experiences
     (physically, mentally, emotionally, spiritually)
       and of our desire and our intentional studies.
         We are slowly synthesized over time.
           We sparkle, like Zirconias!

We are also free. We are wild, instinctively wild.
   We grow where our seeds land—where the wind carries them.

And with our inborn determination and grit, we grow strong and hardy.
   Our beauty 'becomes' with each passing day.
      We are beautiful, wild and free, like Zinnias!

Put on your whimsical poet's hat,
   and look for a moment at your own life, in metaphor.
      What of you, is self-made, synthesized, achieved by goals?
         What of you, sparkles in the Light?
            What of you, radiates beauty, and color and wildness?
               What of you, naturally pleases and delights?

Picture a bouquet of multicolored Zinnias,
   standing in a tall glass vase.
      Now picture at the base of the vase,
         on the wooden mahogany table,
            a handful of 3 carat Zirconias just casually laying there,
               strewn in the sunlight, in full sparklescence.

Attune more closely now,
   and notice that there is no water in the vase,
      but, that it is filled with hundreds of large crystal Zirconias!
         Such a sight to see—
            such incredible natural beauty arising from the Light within!
            Such an image to reflect upon.
               Such a metaphor to use in your own life!

Return to Zirconias and Zinnias every once in a while,
   and let yourself go deep,
      and reflect upon you.
         Wholehearted You, in the Light!

Z

Zumba!

Dear God hear my prayer—my fervent and energetic closing prayer!

Zumba—Columbian slang for 'buzzing like a bee', or fast moving.
   I am energized. I am enlivened. I am on a pathway, a journey,
     that is both rewarding and affirming.
       I am buzzing like a bee,
         full of fire and fervor for Wholehearted Me!
           I am a Zumba leader, on caffeine!

And, I am not alone in my Zumba class. You God, are here with me.
   In every exuberant 'shimmy shimmy shake',
     'cha cha cha', and
       'Arriba!'
         you are here.
           And I love this!
             I love our Zumba-ful Life!

I love who I am, who I'm becoming,
   and who I'll soon become.

Wholeheartedness is no longer simply a notion, or a concept to me.
   It is a way of living. It is a way of being.
     It is an energized life—a fully engaged life,
       where I can explore, release, become, affirm, and transform.
         I can befriend, advocate, empower and serve.
           And I can do all of this in respect—
             in love and in compassion.

I cannot sum it all up in one closing prayer,
   but the word Zumba keeps coming back to me.

I vow to continue to be deeply engaged
   on my journey into Wholehearted Living.
     I vow to eat, drink and breathe Wholeheartedness
       in all of my daily living.
         I vow to share the wonders of My Wholehearted Life,
           broadly, earnestly and with conviction,
             with all who will listen.

WHOLEHEARTED ME A-Z!

My heart is overflowing with gratitude, for all of my recent learning,
   for all of my fresh new perspectives and insights,
     for all of the wisdom arising—erupting—within me!

I am on a pathway, an odyssey,
   of personal growth, and spiritual formation,
     and especially, of affirmation.
       I have a grand *joie de vivre*
         in this time, here and now.
           I have Zumba-zest and Zumba-zeal
              second to none. *Arriba!!!*

I now know what Wholehearted Living
   looks like, sounds like, and feels like.
     I will move forward, toward, onward,
       trusting in your guidance, trusting in your presence,
         trusting that all will be well
           in my newfound Wholehearted Life. Amen!

Closing Prayer

My Wholehearted Prayer—

My Daily Petition to God of My Heart

Please God,

As I awaken to the wonders of this new day,
   grant me the courage, the strength and the grace—
      to become—
         to become more/most fully human—
            to become the engaging, vibrant and enlivened child of God
               that you would have me be—
            to become
               the loving and compassionate servant
                  that you have called me to be—

to stand justly, breathe kindness, and walk humbly with you in my heart,
   in all of my ways, in all of my days.

May my eyes be opened.
   May I see, across the waters and beyond.
      May I see, with the eyes of my heart.

May my glass be half-full, and yet,
   let my cup overflow.

May I know wisdom.
   May I know love.
      May I know you, God.

And as the day unfolds before me,
   please grace me with the warmth of your Holy Lovelight,
      to encourage me—to lead me and to guide me.

Wholehearted Me A-Z!

And in the fullness of each moment, in my here and in my now,
   please walk with me in the Wholehearted Life,
      that I may ever feel and ever know your very real presence-with-me,
         that I may see all life and all living as Sacred,
           that I may ever, always and freely,
              reverence the Sacred in all life and in all living.

And in the quiet and the stillness of day's end,
   when the setting sun and the rising moon and the first star's light
      all share space in the same wide open sky, please grant me peace—

your peace of the endless running waves lapping on the shores—
   your peace of the vastness of the starlit night—
      your peace that passes all understanding—
         your blessed gift of peace.

May I learn, may I grow, may I become.
   May my Wholehearted Life make me whole.
      I pray that your ways be my ways, God.
         Let my Wholehearted Life quietly and surely
           lead others to you—to your Light.

Let my Wholehearted Life be a blessing,
   as you have been such a blessing to me.

Dear God of my heart, please hear my humble prayer. Amen.

Suggested Reading

Brené Brown, *The Gifts of Imperfection* Hazelden Publishing, Center City MN, 2010
Brené Brown, *Daring Greatly*, Penguin Random House, New York, 2012
Brené Brown, *Rising Strong*, Random House, New York, 2017
Brené Brown, *Braving the Wilderness*, Random House, New York, 2019
Brené Brown, *Atlas of the Heart*, Penguin Random House, New York, 2021

Janis Constable, *Random and Nebulous—Nuancing the Psalms,* Resource Publications Wipf and Stock Publishing, Eugene OR, 2021
Janis Constable, *Light Beyond the River*, Resource Publications Wipf and Stock Publishing, Eugene OR, 2022
Janis Constable, *My Indulgent Interior Life*, Resource Publications Wipf and Stock Publishing, Eugene OR, 2023

Esther De Waal, *The Celtic Way of Prayer*, Bantam Doubleday Dell Publishing Group, New York, 1997

Rachel Held Evans, *Wholehearted Faith*, HarperCollins, New York, 2022

John Philip Newell, *Listening for the Heartbeat of God*, Paulist Press, New Jersey, 1997
John Philip Newell, *The Book of Creation*, Paulist Press, New Jersey, 1999
John Philip Newell, *Sacred Earth, Sacred Soul*, HarperCollins, New York, 2021

Henri Nouwen, *The Wounded Healer*, Doubleday Random House, New York, 1972
Henri Nouwen, *The Way Of the Heart*, Random House Publishing Group, 1981

Suggested Reading

Henri Nouwen, *In My Own Words*, Liguori Publications, Liguori MO, 2001

John O'Donohue, *Beauty – The Invisible Embrace*, HarperCollins, New York, 2005

John O'Donohue, *To Bless the Space Between Us*, Penguin Random House, New York, 2008

John O'Donohue, *Walking in Wonder*, Penguin Random House, New York, 2015

Koshin Paley-Ellison, *Wholehearted*, Wisdom Publications, Somerville MA, 2019

Richard Rohr, *Falling Upward—A Spirituality for the Two Halves of Life*, Jossey-Bass, A Wiley Imprint, 2013

Richard Rohr, *The Naked Now—Learning to See as the Mystics See*, Crossroad Publishing, 2018

Stephen Sims, *River of Awareness*, Novalis, Toronto, 2009

Steve Taylor, *The Meaning*, John Hunt Publishing, CPI Group Croydon UK, 2012

Steve Taylor, *The Calm Center*, New World Library Publishing, Novato CA, 2015

Steve Taylor, *The Clear Light*, New World Library Publishing, Novato CA, 2020

The Ravenwolf, *Radiance Rising*, Hyperbole Publications, Boston, 2021

The Ravenwolf, *The Lightbringer – Unbridled*, Hyperbole Publications, Boston, 2021

Eckhart Tolle, *The Power of Now—A Guide to Spiritual Enlightenment*, Namaste Publishing, Vancouver BC, 1997

Eckhart Tolle, *Stillness Speaks*, New World Library, Novato CA, 2003

Eckhart Tolle, *A New Earth—Awakening Your Life's Purpose*, Penguin Life, 2008

Richard Wagamese, *What Comes from Spirit*, Douglas and McIntyre, Madeira Park BC CA, 2021

About the Author

Janis is poetic by nature, and a deeply contemplative thinker, and she's been this way for most of her life. She has written a few books along the way, both fiction and prose poetry, showcasing her contemplative works.

Janis is Canadian—Ontario-born with strong Celtic and maritime family roots. She was raised in the Christian household, and she currently identifies as a modern Celtic Christian. She graduated from the School of Celtic Consciousness, which was founded and taught by renowned author and Celtic Wisdom scholar, John Philip Newell. Janis received her Bachelors Degree in Physical and Health Education from the University of Toronto. Professionally, she served in Emergency Nursing for 33 years, and for 10 years in Parish Nursing Ministry. She is happily married and living with her husband, Barry, in Barrie, Ontario.

Janis' writing career began when she retired from nursing. Her published titles include

Random and Nebulous—Nuancing the Psalms
Voice of the Celtic Christian Contemplative Soul in Prose and in Prayer

Light Beyond the River—
Encountering the Sacred from the Center to the Edge

My Indulgent Interior Life—Seasons of the Deep
Contemplative Prose Poetry Ending with Amen

Wholehearted Me A-Z !
Expressions of Wholehearted Living
in Story, Prosetry and Prayer

ABOUT THE AUTHOR

Janis also wrote *Buddy's Daughter in Soulscape*, and she is still deliberating 'to publish or not to publish'. This is a compilation of her own colorful *Story, Commentary and Affirmations of a Life Well-Lived*, containing sensitive yet exquisitely informative testimonials, teachings and truths.

Please check out her author website for more book details, endorsements and praise, sales information, and especially the Celtic Wisdom musings in her Blog.

The title of Janis' Blog is "Running Wave Contemplative", and it is prefaced by these words . . . .

As the running waves perpetually lap upon the shores
—intrepid, placid and sure—
so too may our thoughts turn to God—
God of Light—God of Love—God of all our hearts.

The website Learning Pages for each book contain questions for study group discussions. The Learning Pages can also be used by individual readers seeking to gain a deeper understanding of Janis' contemplative content.

www.janisconstablebooks.com

Bibliography

Brown, Brené, *Atlas of the Heart*, (New York, Penguin Random House, 2021) p 184
Brown, Brené, *Gifts of Imperfection*, (Center City Minnesota, Hazelden, 2010) p 125
Constable, Janis, *Random and Nebulous—Nuancing the Psalms*, (Eugene Oregon, Wipf and Stock, 2021) p 6, 10, 12, 177
Held-Evans, Rachel, *Wholehearted Faith,* (New York New York, HarperCollins, 2022), p 53, 54
United Church of Canada, *The Manual—A Statement of Faith—A New Creed,* (Toronto, United Church Publishing House, 2023) p 25

www.ingramcontent.com/pod-product-compliance
Lightning Source LLC
Chambersburg PA
CBHW071723090426
42738CB00009B/1855